ON THE FRONT LINE

ON THE FRONT LINE

Clive and Gavin Calver

MONARCH
B O O K S

Oxford, UK & Grand Rapids, Michigan, USA

First published in the UK in 2007 by Monarch Books
(a publishing imprint of Lion Hudson plc),
Mayfield House, 256 Banbury Road, Oxford, OX2 7DH.
Tel: +44 (0) 1865 302750   Fax: +44 (0) 1865 302757
Email: monarch@lionhudson.com
www.lionhudson.com

ISBN: 978-1-85424-790-2 (UK)
ISBN: 978-0-8254-6148-4 (USA)

Distributed by:
UK: Marston Book Services Ltd, PO Box 269,
Abingdon, Oxon OX14 4YN;
USA: Kregel Publications, PO Box 2607,
Grand Rapids, Michigan 49501.

The text paper used in this book has been made from wood
independently certified as having come from sustainable forests.

British Library Cataloguing Data
A catalogue record for this book is available
from the British Library.

Printed and bound in Great Britain by Cox & Wyman Ltd, Reading.

Acknowledgements

We both wanted to express our sincere appreciation to those who have contributed to this book. Particular thanks must go to our wives, Ruth and Anne, for their patience, support and encouragement. Gavin is grateful to many people in the UK who have shown him so much of what it means to live all out for Jesus; especially Roy Crowne, Alex and Flora Buchanan, Jon Burns and Andy Ward. In the USA, Clive would like to thank the elders and friends at Walnut Hill including Clay and Joy Norman, Carol Pious and Leslie Goodwin, whose help has been invaluable in this book. Thanks to those who have supported and loved us in so many ways at our churches: Stanmore Baptist Church, Fatherless Barn Evangelical Church and Walnut Hill Community Church. We would also like to thank all at Monarch for their tireless support and help in this project. For the support of friends we are grateful, they have eradicated many mistakes — but those that remain are all ours!

Contents

Foreword

It **was one hundred years ago** that two movements emerged in America that would change the character of Christianity from being a staid, ecclesiastical institution into a dynamic movement facilitating social change and promising the world a holistic Christianity that had the power, not only to transform individuals, but also to transform society.

The one movement was initiated in Azusa, California, where a handful of Christians prayed for a "breakthrough" of the Holy Spirit that would revitalise a Christianity that had become morbid, and would facilitate a worldwide evangelistic movement. This, of course, was the Pentecostal/Charismatic movement. From that humble beginning, the movement spread around the world. Today there are over 600,000,000 Christians who can trace their brand of spirituality back to the Azusa Street prayer meetings. The movement is having an awesome response around the world. While having a dynamic presence in the United States and the United Kingdom, other parts of the world are undergoing explosive, magnificent revivals. In Africa, 50,000 new Christians are baptised into the church every week. The number is even larger in Latin America, and larger still in Asia. Harvey Cox, the Harvard scholar, has predicted that by the middle of the 21st century it may be the only form of Christianity that has any vitality worth mentioning.

The other movement of great significance, which was

born almost at the same time, was called the Social Gospel. It had its most articulate proponent in Walter Rauschenbusch, who in 1907 published his book, *Christianity and the Social Crisis*. That book, and the discussions and reactions that followed, made Christians around the world aware that the central theme of scripture was the declaration by Jesus that the kingdom of God was at hand. It was Rauschenbusch and his thinking that proved to be a remedy to the "pie-in-the-sky, by-and-by" Christianity which sought simply to get people ready to live in the next world, while regarding this world as having little significance or importance. It was Rauschenbusch who taught Christians to recognise that when we pray the Lord's Prayer, we are praying for the kingdom of God to come on earth as it is in heaven. For Rauschenbusch, true Christianity involved a call to transform the social structures of our society from what they are, into what God wills them to be. Only then, he contended, would God's will be done on earth as it is in heaven. Rauschenbusch longed for a church whose people would invade every institution, bringing to bear the values of Christ which were so brilliantly articulated in the Sermon on the Mount. He wanted the church to be even as Christ called it to be, the leaven and salt that would permeate society and facilitate its transformation. Sadly, in the early part of the 20th century, it was only the extreme liberal wing of the church that caught on to what Rauschenbusch was saying while the Fundamentalist movement, in reaction, would have nothing to do with Rauschenbusch's challenges and beliefs and argued that his "social gospel" was a deviation from the only real calling of the church, which was to evangelise the lost.

Fortunately, in the middle of the 20th century, a prominent Evangelical theologian by the name of Carl Henry came on the scene and with his book, *The Uneasy Conscience of Modern Fundamentalism*, made it clear that biblically based Christianity transcended the either/or mindset that contended that we must either be about winning souls to Christ or transforming the social order. What Carl Henry made clear was that the Bible teaches a holistic Christianity that requires both of these tasks to be taken seriously. For Carl Henry, the kingdom of God, which he saw in accord with Rauschenbusch as being a legitimate goal to be sought in this world, could only be brought about if people were personally transformed by the Gospel and made, through the power of the Holy Spirit, into agents of change. The kingdom of God, according to Henry, would result from transformed people joining up with a God who was at work in the world, transforming social structures into institutions that reflected love and justice.

All of this is a prelude to saying that in this book, you will read about a father and a son who recognise the validity of both of these movements and bring them together in personal lifestyles aimed at being the people and doing the things that Carl Henry so strongly advocated a little over fifty years ago.

While not necessarily identifying themselves as Pentecostals, they do recognise that unless the Holy Spirit infuses individuals with the energy and love that only God's Spirit can generate, there won't be any hope for the creation of a church empowered to be relevant in addressing the social needs of the world. With clarity, the authors advocate a church that wins individuals to Christ and is relevant to the social needs of our time. They want a church that is equipped intellectually to engage the secular community in discussion and debate in meaningful and creative ways.

What Clive and Gavin make abundantly clear, is that the kind of Christianity prescribed by scripture and inspired by the Holy Spirit is more than the easy "believism" that often exists in our churches today. They recognise that too often we have called people Christians simply because they have given intellectual assent to certain propositional statements. They demonstrate that affirming creeds and doctrines is not enough. Clive and Gavin make that very clear. They contend that a relevant church will require radical discipleship and refuse to water down the hard sayings of Christ as he calls us to sacrifice all and become his followers. They make it clear that Jesus never called us to go into all the world and make believers out of everyone, but instead called us to make disciples out of everyone. And they make it clear that there is a big difference between believers and disciples.

It is a call to discipleship that is at the core of this book. The authors contend that anything less than people who are ready to surrender their lives and all they have to meet the needs of others, spiritually and socially, is less than what we are called to do and be. While recognising that salvation comes by *grace* and not by works, they go on to point out that while we are not saved by good works, we are certainly saved for good works. When reading the words of this father and son combination, you will be led to the awareness that to be Christian requires commitments to share the Gospel story, but at the same time to work for social justice. Clive and Gavin challenge Christians to leave behind that "politically correct" type of religiosity that is reluctant to talk about Jesus in the public sector for fear that others might be offended, and they reject with vehemence any attempt to make Christianity into an enclave detached from the sufferings of the world. These two men have a special heart for the poor and the oppressed. Clive Calver served for several years as President of World Concern, one of the largest faith-based relief programs in the world today.

Gavin Calver, on the other hand, has travelled with his father to third world countries and experienced the sufferings of that half of the world's population living on less than £1.00 ($2.00) a day. Working with Youth for Christ, Gavin has propagated the holistic Gospel that brings together the enthusiasm of Pentecostalism with the social conscience of the Social Gospel movement.

These two men have made an impact for Christ and the kingdom on both sides of the Atlantic and are brilliant examples of a balanced, holistic Christianity that synthesises the best insights that have emerged from scripture over the last hundred years. Transcending pietistic legalism, they offer to the reader a vision of what it means to be fully alive in Christ in the 21st century.

Tony Campolo, PhD.
Professor of Sociology
Eastern University, St Davids, PA. USA

SECTION ONE

Follow That Dream

CHAPTER ONE

Only Half a Christian? (Clive)

The waitresses in the restaurant were not quite sure what to make of the situation. After all, here was a twenty-three-year-old guy, who had just eaten a hearty breakfast, suddenly shedding great teardrops that were now rapidly covering the table. All the same, he did not appear to be terribly sad, and his companion appeared to be pretty comfortable with the proceedings. Any one of the staff in that diner on that day could have been forgiven for asking the question, 'So, what on earth was going on?'

The answer would probably have amazed them. The main event was not taking place down on earth. At that moment heaven would have been a pretty excited place. What was happening here? After years of searching and internal struggle, Ryan was finally surrendering his life to Jesus Christ.

Within just nine months, he found himself on a plane and heading for Bangladesh in order to serve Jesus among the tiny minority of Christians in that country. To the churches there, Ryan was coming to join them as a much-needed reinforcement. The son of an elder in the church back home, he would have plenty of opportunity to grow in his new found faith within the Bangladeshi churches.

For Bangladeshi Christians, he would be the first English teacher the children ever had who spoke English as his first language. For Ryan himself, he was living out the implications of the initial commitment he had made as he prayed through the tears at that diner table, when he acknowledged that anything less than a Christianity which challenged and transformed his life was simply unacceptable.

So was this his attempt to earn salvation? No, of course not. None of us can ever earn or deserve the life of Christ living within us. Such a rebirth comes as the result of crucified love alone. Nor can we expect that surrendering to Christ could ever mean less than the daily progressive transformation of our lives, in order to resemble our lord and king more closely. We were never intended to live the same kind of life that we had before we met Christ, just with regular prayer, church attendance and Bible reading added on! The call of Christ is never to remain content, to stay the same as we were, but daily to be changed by his grace and power.

Once we come to Christ, our destiny lies in his hands rather than our own. (He challenges us because he has always been there to comfort the disturbed, but also to disturb the comfortable.) He is not only equipping us to survive here on planet earth until the day comes when he can transport us to glory. Instead, Jesus sees his church composed of those he can use to challenge and change his world.

Contrary to what many of us may have been taught to expect, he does not call us to the comfortable maintenance of the status quo, with Jesus added on to guarantee our safety and well-being; instead, he offers us an introduction to his adventure in 'risky' living. This is not life without a purpose, but the exact opposite. It is life with a purpose that we might not have chosen for ourselves. A purpose like Bangladesh, to teach poor and orphaned kids to speak English, and find both Jesus and a future.

Now that we know our lives are not our own, we can expect to be redirected into pathways we could never have anticipated, or necessarily designed for ourselves. For we now live with different motivation, under new management, and not in our own strength – but through faith and trust in the Supreme One who gave his life for us.

The idea that life in Christ will simply make us mild and inoffensive is clearly ridiculous. A message of crucified love needs to be lived and not just talked about. It has to be worked out in practice. If our faith is ever to be real, then it should be no more painless to us than it was for Christ. It clearly has to cost something.

In today's world, to conceive of a Christian faith without sacrifice is about as imaginable, relevant, consistent and worthwhile as a Christ without a cross. Ryan wanted a faith that would challenge him to the depths of his being, and he found one when he surrendered his life to Jesus Christ.

The King and his Kingdom

'But I want it!' The three-year-old toddler gazes longingly at the toy in the shop window, plaintively screaming at his mother as she drags him away. So also we each know how to demand whatever takes our fancy.

We live in an acquisitive society. 'Get what you can' has become a commonplace desire of life. What may be harder to tell is how much we are prepared to sacrifice to obtain the object of our current desire. Or to put it more bluntly – what price are we prepared to pay?

The mere idea that there might be personal cost involved in getting what we want is often foreign to our thinking. However, this was certainly not true of Jesus. He taught that admission into the kingdom of heaven was the greatest thing that anyone could ever achieve. So he announced, 'Come, you who are blessed by my Father; take your inheritance, the kingdom prepared for you since the creation of the world' (Matthew 25:34).

We cannot earn our entrance fee into this kingdom, nor can we ever deserve to be there, but still there is always a cost attached. For life in the kingdom resembles hidden treasure deposited in a field, and 'When a man found it, he hid it again, and then in his joy went and sold all he had and bought that field' (Matthew 13:44). Or it is like a pearl of great price, which is worth selling all you own in order to buy it (Matthew 13:45–46).

This kingdom is available to those who are born again, gentle in spirit, and prepared to 'keep going' (Luke 9:62; John 3:3; Matthew 5:3). Such people may seem to be poor in the eyes of the world, but they are certainly 'rich in faith' (James 2:5).

So, what on earth is this kingdom? When Jesus taught his disciples to pray, he employed Hebrew parallelism, as in the psalms. In other words, he said the same thing twice. Nowadays many of us preachers go one step further and repeat ourselves three times. But Jesus asked for God's kingdom to come, and then immediately requested of his Father, 'Your will be done on earth as it is in heaven' (Matthew 6:10).

Simply put, that is the kingdom. It is wherever the will of God is performed on earth, as it is in heaven. It is therefore two-dimensional in character. It is fulfilled in part now, and it will be perfectly fulfilled later. For a kingdom requires a king – and when Jesus arrived proclaiming the gospel (or good news) of the kingdom (Matthew 4:23), the kingdom dawned on humankind. In one sense, the kingdom fully arrived with the presence of the King, but then he went away again! However, he will be back, and when the King of kings returns it will be to establish his reign in our lives forever (Revelation 17:14).

Sometimes a ruler, whether it is a monarch or a president, can seem awfully remote. But the incredible news of this king is that he wants to be loved and known by us personally. So even a dying thief could gaze wistfully into the immediate future and reflect on what it would mean to be remembered by Jesus when the Christ entered into his kingdom (Luke 23:42).

In the scriptures, Jesus is revealed as the King of kings, Lord of lords, Son of God, Word of God, and saviour of the world. I love to talk in the language of the intimacy of personal relationship. 'My Jesus' is therefore a statement of deeply felt affection and gratitude rather than glib familiarity. However, we must never allow the depth of feeling to obscure the glorious majesty of who he is.

Because I so often talk of him as 'Jesus', I suppose it was inevitable that one day I would receive a letter of rebuke from an elderly Christian rightly insisting that the total biblical name is 'The Lord Jesus Christ'. That is true. But that title is more than just a name. In the Hebrew mindset often the name selected was intended to reveal something of the identity, character and authority of the person who bore it.

Certainly in the New Testament, Christ's saviourhood (his role in bringing us forgiveness, redemption and reconciliation with God) is always joined to his lordship – he *is* both saviour and lord.

However, we have short memories for things that we might not necessarily like. Jesus as saviour is wonderful, but as lord and king he might interfere with things that we do not want to have to refer to him. So the tendency today has often been to over-emphasise Christ's role as saviour at the expense of his lordship. If we believe that way, it makes for an easier and more comfortable life – but then, compromise usually does.

How like the rest of the world we can easily be? We like the good and easy parts, but try to ignore the painful and the sacrificial. To preach Jesus Christ as saviour without equally emphasising his lordship may be popular – but it is totally unbiblical. And when we do pay casual lip service to the word 'lord', it usually passes without further explanation.

The same applies to our response to his right to reign in our lives. We often seek to limit his authority to the abstract realm of cosmic kingship. We can freely sing the words, 'Reign in me, Sovereign Lord, reign in me', but rarely do we reflect on their true meaning. For the ultimate cost of true discipleship lies in this proposition: for King Jesus to reign in us, we must first abdicate the throne of our own lives. Only then can he fully live and reign as king – in us.

Additionally, this assertion affirms the truth that we need to be careful not to glibly say something with our lips that is not echoed in our hearts and lives. To own Christ as king and to fully participate in his kingdom will mean returning to the revelation of a twentieth-century prophetic spokesman, Malcolm Muggeridge, who discovered what so many have missed:

> So I came back to where I began, to that other King, one Jesus; to the Christian notion that man's efforts to make himself personally and collectively happy in earthly terms are doomed to failure. He must indeed, as Christ said, be born again, be as a new man or he's nothing. So at least I have concluded, having failed to find in the past experience, present dilemmas and future expectations, any alternative proposition. As far as I am concerned, it is Christ or nothing.[1]

The God who Takes Over

Sometimes I wonder if the rich young ruler really got a pretty raw deal at the hands of Jesus. The demand to give everything can certainly come over as being quite unreasonable. And what is the big problem with his being so attached to material possessions anyway? Is asking that young man to relinquish them similar to us being challenged to give up on sporting involvements or career plans? Surely God could never do that! After all, he does want the best for us, doesn't he? And only we ourselves can know what the demand to give all entails.

Sadly, we have been content to develop a very comfortable view of God. He has to remain extraordinarily well-behaved and not rock our boat too often.

Yet crucified love declares that God salvages the individual by liquidating him and then raising him again to newness of life. He offers a different kind of life, not a rehash of the old one. In other words, God offers real life, but not an improved old life. The life he died to bring to us, by definition, is life out of death. It stands always on the far side of the cross.

That summary is the best I know of the gospel we are in danger of losing, and of the terrible price we are paying for losing it. John the Baptist found himself ministering to a very similar society. Israel emphasised offer at the expense of demand. They claimed a spiritual pedigree, suggesting that the demand had been adequately fulfilled by their ancestor, Abraham. Now all that was required of contemporary Israelites was to receive the promises at no extra cost to themselves.

We can all fall into the very same trap today. Much of our message emphasises 'offers' because we are afraid to mention 'demand' in our postmodern world, thinking that would only serve to put people off. We forget that people seek reality today rather than cheap and substandard imitations. In this area, the evangelist most resembles the door-to-door salesman – 'Do you want love, joy, peace, etc.? Come to Jesus.' That message can never be the total gospel. It must be balanced by the demands involved.

Too often we have been content to engage in a subtle sell-out, sacrificing the full scale all-out message of Jesus for the sake of our own popularity. Unlike Jesus, we have wanted respectability and acceptance within our community.

Imagine what it would be like if some modern-day evangelists met the rich young ruler. My guess is that he would never have been allowed to walk away. Instead, we would run after him and offer 50 per cent, or even 10 per cent of his life in return for his decision. We could always rationalise our compromise with the comforting assertion that the Bible talks much of a tithe! We would then consider that he was guaranteed eternal life!

Jesus knew that there could be no such reduction in the minimum requirements for entry into his kingdom. Thus he simply laid truth on the line and told it like it is.

If we fail to balance our casual offers with the actual demands which Jesus laid down then we may discover that our imaginary gospel ultimately offers little more than an imaginary salvation.

Just Not Enough

What *does* Jesus demand in order that his kingdom might be established in our hearts and lives? How did Jesus preach the good news? He clearly declared the message in uncompromising terms: 'If anyone would come after me, he must deny himself and take up his cross and follow me' (Matthew 16:24). Time and again, Jesus taught a gospel of discipleship, and by that he meant cross-bearing for beginners (Matthew 10:38; Mark 10:21). That concept alone was his message, nothing more, nothing less, and nothing else. We reduce it at our peril.

The German theologian Dietrich Bonhoeffer, who died at the hands of Adolf Hitler in a Second World War concentration camp, often warned against the dangers of 'cheap grace'. Jesus declared that 'anyone who does not carry his cross and follow me cannot be my disciple' (Luke 14:27). That message should be unequivocal enough, but when did we last hear that as a straightforward gospel message? I am forced to the conclusion that, if the message was good enough for Jesus, then we have no right to dilute it. For some things are surely to be regarded as company policy and remain strictly non-negotiable.

Gavin and I had been bouncing around in a poorly equipped SUV for hour after hour, in Ethiopia, where the roads are questionable at the best of times. Finally, our guides found the remote village that we were searching for, and we set out to supply grain and seed to the little church so that they could be able to help the villagers combat the famine – and save the lives of their children.

However, to accomplish our task, we first had to find the church. As usual this was not too difficult. There is something about one member of a family trying to locate another, and familial recognition between Christians is not that different. I found an attractive young African woman with her two beautiful small children playing by her feet, and I asked her who she was.

She wasted no time in telling me that she was actually the pastor's wife, but her husband was away preaching in the next village, telling the people there, who had no church, about Jesus. I was thrilled. Obviously, we had found people who were committed to Christ, who wanted to share his love and his truth, and who could be trusted to distribute life-saving food to the local communities.

She told me that she and her husband had only been in the village for around one year, so just to make conversation, I asked her about the previous pastor in the village.

'Oh, they killed him,' she replied.

Then she explained that he had come preaching about this strange God, this Jesus. But the rain stopped, and the crops died, so the villagers killed him to appease all the other gods who were offended and angry at the village for paying attention to him.

The church was growing. It was now twenty-three people, and no longer just the seven who were there when they had arrived. But the rains had not come, and without help, starvation was not the only thing that threatened.

'So why did you and your husband and the two little children come here?'

She looked at me as if I was an idiot, and replied: 'But we are Christians, this is what Christians do, isn't it?'

Such sacrifice is the result when we abdicate the throne of our own lives and let Jesus reign as king alone. This commitment is, after all, the only possible explanation for that kind of unflinching courage. We may not like to read about the creation of monopolies, but King Jesus will never be satisfied with anything less.

In fact, in this case our heavenly Father is a capitalist – he only believes in takeover bids! God's ultimate glory was, for him, a message worth dying for. To us, it brings a whole new meaning and direction to our lives.

His authority must be shouted from the rooftops. 'Who is he, this King of glory? The Lord Almighty – he is the King of glory' (Psalm 24:10).

We must no longer proclaim a gutless gospel in which Jesus is relegated to the status of 'saviour'. My friend and my saviour is no mere companion, just a 'Gentle Jesus' figure for me to turn to when needed. This Jesus has always demanded that he must be, now and forever, my Lord and my King. If his kingdom rule is to extend into our hearts and lives, then we can afford to be in charge of our lives no longer.

Note

1. Malcolm Muggeridge, *Another King* (St. Andrew Press, 1968)

CHAPTER TWO

An Imaginary
Salvation? (Clive)

Come with me in a flashback to nearly thirty years ago. A bunch of us had been converted; we had given our lives over to Jesus Christ. Many had taken that step during the closing years of the 1960s. Then we had emerged from universities and theological seminaries, but with a passion to see things changed in the United Kingdom — starting with our evangelical churches. We could look back at a century of unremitting decline. Each year evangelical Christians in the UK declined in number and decreased in influence till there were precious few left.

The one exception to the tragic catalogue of reducing numbers had come in 1955, in the aftermath of a major Billy Graham campaign. But now the curve was flattening out. The Baptists were the first major denomination to point to a reduced rate of decline. The possibilities of change hung in the air, but you would have to be a faith-filled optimist to recognise them. The realities of church life and witness must certainly have seemed pretty grim to the post-sixties young Christian.

Let me provide an action replay of an 'alter call' of the period:

Jesus himself is calling out to you tonight. Will you accept him as your saviour and friend? He is patiently waiting at the door of your heart. Why will you not open that door and let him in right now? You know that this could be your time. How long will you reject this wonderful free offer of his love, joy, peace, satisfaction and happiness? All are freely available to you today. You cannot earn them, but you can receive them. All you need to do is to believe in Jesus. Ask him into your heart as we sing this closing hymn. Ask and he'll come right now.

The results in a person's life were often virtually indistinguishable from what had been before. Sincere and concerned individuals prayed the 'sinner's prayer' and added the practices of church attendance, Bible study and prayer on to their old respectable lifestyles. Exceptions to the rule were feted as celebrities with their 'guest testimony' being frequently in demand.

Both in Britain and America, that kind of 'gospel' was proclaimed Sunday after Sunday in hundreds of pulpits. Faithful men, repeating what they had been taught were unwittingly running the risk of misleading people into a cheap and easy 'salvation'. Some were undoubtedly 'conned' by this simple subconscious confidence trick; an invitation to receive what, more often than not, became an imaginary salvation. Others wondered if this was all there actually was to it. But then, at least heaven was now guaranteed, and surely that would be different.

Sadly, when listening to some gospel presentations today we could seriously question whether anything has really changed. I guess that we were failing to understand the full dimensions of the gospel in the past. Are we still living out that failure, and could we be reaping the same results today?

Missing Out on the Message

Recently, I managed to bring a party of Brits and Americans out of Israel at the very time it was becoming a war zone.

My wife Ruth and I arrived home to breathe a sigh of relief. Imagine our delight on arriving at the house to discover that Alan (not his real name), a very competent chef, had not only looked after our Boxer puppy for us – he had also cooked a succulent dinner ready for our return.

Now Alan had been a witch. Formerly a fully-fledged follower of Wicca, he and I met a few weeks after he had given his life to Jesus Christ. I have had the joy of watching his progress. I was there when we burned the books and games and all the paraphernalia of his witchcraft. I've laughed and prayed with him as he has grown up in Christ. I had the thrill of seeing the incredible joy on his face as I baptised him into Jesus and his body.

I have also seen the tears as he privately testified to our elders here at the church of his new-found faith, and of all that he had come out of, and been delivered from. I have watched the pressure as he has learned to serve others despite his own pain. I have seen him wracked with anguish in the process of divorce from a wife who would not leave her witchcraft. And I have observed the struggle that he has gone through, knowing that all he has come from is better left unsaid. But keeping parts of the story quiet has meant that others were therefore not able to appreciate all he has endured.

Each month I have watched the changes in Alan, and they have been little short of spectacular. God is revolutionising the life of a relatively new disciple, bringing forth the fruit of the Holy Spirit. I will continue to enjoy watching an ongoing transformation which lines up so directly with what I believe the Bible teaches about the reality of a spiritual life. I am proud to call Alan a friend.

How did this transformation start? This kind of work of God did not come from Alan just accepting Jesus on his terms. It came from a complete and ongoing surrender of this man's life into the hands of Jesus Christ, so that the Lord could do what he pleased with him. That surrender is a great beginning to a life of discipleship.

Jesus never instructed his followers when he left that they were to 'Go and make converts'. Instead he urged them to 'go and make disciples of all nations'. Then he added that they were to teach these new disciples to 'obey everything I have commanded you' (Matthew 28:19, 20). He also promised to be with them in that task.

Yet how often have we expected long-term disciples, only to end up with short-term converts? I can speak from bitter experience. I remember the time when a friend and I were conducting a mission at which over a hundred young people made decisions for Christ. A year passed, and I returned to the church to preach on the anniversary of the mission. To my horror, only a handful of those who had been 'converted' remained. I would have easily blamed the church for ineffective follow-up, but I had to face up to the fact that the truth could lie closer to home.

Tragically, instead of learning how to communicate *to* our day and generation, we have too often learned *from* it how we can better communicate. Learning to imitate the advertising techniques of our modern-day society may generate an entertaining presentation — but we need to ask what the long-term results actually are. The apostle Paul warned the Corinthian church that the Lord Jesus will test the quality of our work, and its effectiveness (and our ultimate reward) will be measured by whether or not the fruit survives (1 Corinthians 3:13–14).

The evangelist can too quickly descend to the level of a door-to-door salesman of ready-packaged, bargain religion. Such a person can unconsciously resort to convincing any number of folk to receive this 'new birth' by slick selling techniques. The church desires to turn the world upside down, but instead the world has invaded the church – and sometimes in the name of evangelism!

Paul followed up on the churches he planted and the new disciples he left behind. We are entitled to ask why some evangelists today are so reluctant to make return visits. Perhaps we hesitate because where we had expected to see healthy babies, instead we are confronted with the tragedy of innumerable stillbirths. How many spiritual babies are stillborn because we have so often tried to bring the gospel down to their level? Why do we seek to make the gospel acceptable, instead of laying the message out in the uncompromising terms that Jesus always used? These questions are very sobering. Whether standing on a platform or chatting to our friends, we need to come preaching 'the gospel of the kingdom' like Jesus did.

If we are to follow Jesus' example, then our emphasis needs to lie in making disciples rather than obtaining 'results'.

The Lausanne Covenant declared, 'evangelism itself is the proclamation of the historical, biblical Christ as saviour and lord, with a view to persuading people to come to him personally and so be reconciled to God. In issuing the gospel invitation we have no liberty to conceal the cost of discipleship. Jesus still calls all who would follow him to deny themselves, take up their cross and identify themselves with his new community.'[1]

Some years ago, I was invited by a fellow evangelist to address a meeting during a series of events that he was leading in a local town. As I spoke, I was assured by the Lord that three or four people in the hall that night were being challenged by his Spirit. I finished my allotted twenty-minute message on time (somewhat unusual!) by making a brief challenge to any who had felt the hand of God touching their lives, or were just interested in what had been said, to come and talk further afterwards.

The evangelist then proceeded to announce the last song and took the opportunity to reinforce the challenge with an appeal lasting no less than seventeen minutes! This lengthy 'begging' minimised the cost of discipleship, and emphasised the joy and ease of coming to Jesus.

Now appeals are by no means wrong in themselves, but they can be misused in the intensity of the moment. Twenty people responded to that appeal – when I was certain that God had promised three or four. I do hope they survived the crush in the counselling room and met the Lord who had been see them. Furthermore, I trust that the evangelist and I have been forgiven for any overenthusiastic attempt to do God's work for him!

Please forgive me if I offend, and don't get me wrong. I do not doubt either the motivation or good intentions that lie behind such actions. It's just that, as in Alan's case, we need to grasp the spiritual realities which must be involved in a transfer from the kingdom of darkness, in order to fully enter into the kingdom of light. Our eagerness to bring others to Christ can make us reduce the demand that Christ makes upon our lives while increasing the desirability of the offer!

When Ruth and I go shopping, we each have a different focus. She first looks at the quality of a product, while I examine the price tag. Both are necessary, of course, but it is a bit silly to focus entirely on one and not the other.

When we come to faith, a radical transformation in lifestyle is part of the deal. In many ways my problems did not end when I came to Jesus; a lot of them really began. I had found much of my sin to be, if not satisfying, at least enjoyable. Now I had a new lord and king and he expected to be giving the direction in my life – not me!

In the light of all this revelation, we are not surprised that Jesus himself often spoke of false prophets and a false gospel, warning of those who would be shocked to the core when he disowned them at the judgement seat. Perhaps we need to recognise again that Christ's commitment to be our saviour is inextricably linked to the authority we surrender to him to be lord of our lives.

A. W. Tozer, referring to the gospel of his day as 'the discredited doctrines of a divided Christ', also commented 'Christ is both saviour and lord. A sinner may be saved by accepting him as saviour without yielding to him as lord', and he retorted, 'Christ's saviourhood is for ever united to his lordship, Christ must be lord or he will not be saviour.'[2]

It's Only a Matter of Words

One of the problems with language is that it changes. We can feel very secure in knowing what we mean when we use a word or a phrase, but does our hearer understand the same thing we intended? Even we ourselves may be misled into repeating phrases that have lost their original meaning without our realising it.

One example is the way that the King James Bible refers to Holy Spirit as the 'Comforter'. The picture which the seventeenth-century translators envisaged was not that of a sympathetic ear! If we go back in history, we do get a clearer picture of what was actually meant by the word — and the picture is far from comforting!

The Bayeux tapestry, strangely, helps us to understand. It was produced in eleventh-century France to commemorate the Norman invasion of Britain in 1066, and their great victory at the Battle of Hastings. This massive cloth depicts one of Duke William's supporters prodding a Norman soldier, a reluctant hero, into battle with the point of a spear in his rear. Underneath this picture is the poignant comment that King William 'comforteth his soldiers'!

The comfort that the Holy Spirit brings is not an arm around us, but an empowering and equipping to mobilise us for battle. Not content with being our divine counsellor and ever-present guide, this Holy Spirit also is the one who provides resources for us to fulfil all that God wills for us.

His anointing power is not only for the healing of the broken-hearted, but also for the defeat of the enemy. That power actually makes him a great 'Comforter', but not in the style that the word conveys today.

There are other problems that we can get from well-worn words and phrases that mean a lot to us, but may not now have the meaning we originally intended. Take, for example, the phrase 'Accept Jesus as your saviour'. This wording constitutes one of the most common errors among Bible-believing churches today, since it places all the emphasis on the offer, but with little challenge attached. It runs the risk of convincing people that half-hearted Christianity can freely masquerade as the real thing.

The first problem with 'accepting Jesus' is that the phrase is not in scripture, and it almost sounds as if we are doing God a favour by offering him a partnership in our lives. Now I appreciate that the idea of 'accepting' Jesus did start many of us out on our spiritual journey. I also understand that we can invest a word with far more meaning than it offers at first hearing. People can easily be misled into feeling that it is possible to accept the existence or reality of Jesus as the condition for calling themselves a 'Christian'.

This notion is appealing, but sadly it is a fallacy. Apart from the fact that Jesus must be lord in order to be saviour, the concept of us 'accepting' Jesus is ludicrous. It forgets that Jesus Christ – King of kings, Lord of lords, the everlasting King of glory, the holy Son of God – cannot just accept you or me on our own terms.

On the one occasion when 'accept' is used in the Bible, the question asked is not 'Will you accept Jesus?' but 'Will he accept you?' This case is not 'Will the sinner accept the King?' but 'Will the King accept the sinner?'

This difference arises because holiness and sin can never walk meekly together. One must always bow to the other. Jesus can only gladly welcome sinners when they come in repentance, seeking forgiveness, but never when they expect him to bless them in their sin!

On one occasion, I was speaking to a gathering of preachers on this subject when one of them interrupted from the back saying, 'I don't agree. What about these words, "Here I am! I stand at the door and knock. If anyone opens the door, I will come in and eat with him, and he with me" (Revelation 3:20)?'

Revelation 3:20 is the classic proof text for the whole notion of accepting Jesus into your heart. But these words were not written to non-Christians, far from it. In fact, they were addressed to the members of the backslidden church of Laodicea. The picture is not of a weak, feeble Jesus standing at the door of the sinner's heart with the dew glistening in his hair, desperately pleading to be allowed in. For Jesus just does not stand and feebly plead. The true picture is the good shepherd going out and bringing the wanderers back. He goes to find his own backslidden Christians and waits to be allowed to return to his rightful position as lord and king of their lives.

There is a famous picture painted by the nineteenth-century English artist, Holman Hunt, depicting Jesus holding a lantern in the undergrowth, knocking on a door. This artwork has often been used to illustrate the so-called 'deeper points' of Revelation 3:20. Actually the painting is based upon Jesus talking about himself as 'the light for the world' (John 8:12). He called men and women to leave their own darkness and join with him in illuminating the world with the light of his life!

We know scripture can have a dual meaning, and there could be a secondary application for non-Christians in Revelation 3:20 – but only if it is considered in its context. What then is the last word of Revelation 3:19? Few people can answer that question. In fact, the word is 'repent' and it is the forgotten word in our evangelistic vocabulary.

Our message must never be reduced to the level of 'easy acceptance' without true repentance or 'turning around' in our lifestyle, and genuine commitment. When Paul talked about 'accepting', he urged us in his letter to the church at Rome to offer our bodies as a living sacrifice to God – that would be acceptable to him because it would be a 'spiritual act of worship' (Romans 12:1).

So here we have it, the idea of accepting Jesus is only a valid concept when applied to his standards and attributes, not to his personality. The previous mistaken view has resulted in a whole new generation of Christians that has come into contemporary society believing that they can 'accept' Christ without forsaking the world. The real question is not if we will accept Jesus, but whether or not he wants us. Don't worry! The answer is an unequivocal 'YES', but on his terms and not ours. Jesus clearly spelled it out when he said that life with him was conditional on us denying ourselves, taking up our cross, and following him. Those conditions were the non-negotiable entrance fee to the life of discipleship.

In this way, Jesus died to show us how to come to God, not just through an easy acceptance of who he is but by the crucifixion of our old life and resurrection into a new way of living. When we adopt his lifestyle, his Spirit begins to live a new life implanted in us.

What Kind of Commitment?

So what does this new lifestyle mean? Simply that the Lord will not accept the role of junior partner in our lives. As the Lord of glory, he demands nothing less than a fully-fledged commitment of our whole being to him.

Some may want to respond that the apostle Paul only told the jailor in Philippi that he had to 'Believe in the Lord Jesus, and you will be saved' (Acts 16:31). Now that little word 'believe' has certainly caused more than its fair share of problems. For years, this word was used to convey the very heart of the Christian gospel, yet in recent times, it has gained a variety of meanings which lead to confusion.

My father was a Christian, and many years ago I asked him, coming from a very different generation, what the word 'believe' meant to him.

'That's easy,' was the reply. 'It means a total and complete surrender of your life to Jesus Christ, recognising that he died because he loved you, and asking him to share his life with you by living in you as your lord and saviour.'

That answer is, of course, completely correct. But nowadays, 'believe' has acquired the general meaning of an intellectual acceptance, a basic recognition of certain facts, rather than a radical commitment to a changed lifestyle. Let's face it, even the devil believes that there is a God. In the same way, he believes in Jesus, in that he cannot deny his existence. But whoever thought that made Satan a Christian?

For most Christians, these words are indelibly imprinted on our memory banks: 'For God so loved the world that he gave his one and only Son, that whoever believes in him shall not perish but have eternal life' (John 3:16). Yet for too many today that word 'believes' can easily mean a mere intellectual acceptance of the life and death of Jesus. It is only a short step from there to think that this head knowledge equals conversion and that no radical change in our lifestyle or perspective is required. However, that is not the New Testament position.

Real belief is so much more than a mere mental acceptance of the existence of an historical Jesus. Nor can belief be reduced to the simple mental acceptance of a set of doctrinal propositions. Greek can be a complicated language because often words like 'love' or 'believe' have more than one meaning, and in Greek there is often one word for each separate meaning. For this reason, Dr Alan Richardson writes, 'In the context of men's relation to God the verb (to believe – *pisteuo*) always implies a personal conviction and trust arising within a direct personal relationship. The New Testament Greek reflects this point by introducing a preposition ('believe in...'). Obedience and conformity to what God prescribes is the inevitable concomitant of believing.'[3]

For the writers of the New Testament, the call to believe was a call to discipleship. It meant total surrender to Jesus with all the ethical demands that this involved. It was far more than an intellectual belief in the divinity of Christ, or in some doctrine of atonement.

True belief is the opening of a life to Jesus in simple trust and commitment. Then he can enter our lives and take full control and authority. He comes into us to reign, so perhaps the best way to describe our response to him lies in the word 'surrender'. In other words we rescind our own self-government and surrender to his rule and reign in us. After all, total lordship is the right position for the one who is Saviour, God and King of kings.

The Bible has made it quite clear that the faith which

comes from true believing must always be joined together with obedience. Thus you can always tell true belief because it leads a person to obey Jesus with the totality of his life.

Being critical and negative is always easier than being positive and constructive. We need to regain a balance in our presentation of the gospel between its two major con-stituents – demand and offer. Of course, Christianity involves the 'offer' of resurrection, but surely it pre-sup-poses the 'demand' of being crucified. For too long, we have relished the offer and denied the demand. We want to be saved, but we stubbornly insist that Christ does all of the dying, while we do all the living. Instead of leading people to a cross, too often we encourage them to live in the strength of their dying self, while asking for his blessing to be upon them.

An older man of God, who merited the title of a twenti-eth-century prophet, taught me what it meant to live the crucified life when he was once asked by a young Christian, 'What does it mean to be crucified?' The answer was very direct. He replied that it meant three things – the crucified man is facing in only one direction, he's not going back, and he has no further plans of his own.

Today, what seems to be a largely 'uncrucified' genera-tion lacks that kind of single-mindedness. If only we stopped looking back longingly at some of our old ways. If only we said goodbye to a lost life, and were content with his plans for our new life, rather than our own plans – then so much would be different.

Let us allow A.W. Tozer to speak for himself. 'All unan-nounced and mostly undetected, there has come in modern times a new cross into popular evangelical circles. From this cross has sprung a new philosophy of the Christian life, and from the new philosophy has come a new evangelical technique – a new type of meeting and a new kind of preaching... The new cross does not slay the sinner, it redirects him. It gears him into a cleaner and jollier way of living and saves his self-respect.'[4]

Comments like these encourage us to pause and draw breath, to ask if we should stop presenting the Christian life as so easy that it can seem contemptible. Rather than attracting people with our 'easy' gospel, we have sometimes merely succeeded in repelling them.

Many will join hands today in affirming that the time has come for an unequivocal commitment to what the Bible says, rather than what we want it to say. The price tag for returning to this biblical truth will involve the complete rejection of a substandard faith that frankly owes more to the norms of our culture and to the current whims and vagaries of our own evangelical imaginations!

When we regain the message *of* Jesus, and not just *about* Jesus, then our Western world will begin to listen again. The Lord Jesus stated the truth clearly when he declared the fact that 'Anyone who does not carry his cross and follow me cannot be my disciple', and as if to rub salt into the wound, he added, 'Any of you who does not give up everything he has cannot be my disciple' (Luke 14:27, 33). That message is worth returning to, and – could I add – it alone is worthy of living and dying for. This is the kingdom God seeks to create on earth.

Notes

1. John Stott et al, *International Congress on World Evangelization* (Lausanne, 1974).
2. A. W. Tozer, *The Best of A. W. Tozer*, (Grand Rapids, Baker Books, 1978).
3. Alan Richardson, *A Theological Word Book of the Bible* (Norwich, SCM Press, 1963).
4. A. W. Tozer, *ibid.*

CHAPTER THREE

The Way It Is (Gavin)

ate one Sunday afternoon, I arrived home from preaching. I was just beginning to sink into the sofa to watch a film when the phone rang. It was a well-known, reputable, national radio station calling to see if I would go on their evening show. Normally I love doing their live phone-ins but it had been rather a long day and I was pretty tired. I would have been more than happy just to stay at home and relax. After all, the only role for an evangelical Christian on such programmes is to serve as a lamb for the slaughter.

This is secular broadcasting so you just put yourself out there and then they tie you down in such a way as to make you appear irrelevant, archaic and discredited. However, when the caller explained that the evening discussion was titled 'Why is the church so irrelevant?' I felt compelled to accept the invitation. Dead lamb walking or not I willingly agreed to head for the slaughterhouse. The reason being that I'm fed up with the church constantly being kicked by an increasingly secular society and a topic like this is hot on my agenda.

Sitting in a small cramped holding area, waiting to go on national radio between 10 p.m. and 12 a.m. on a Sunday night is not half as glamorous as you might think! I always spend the time pondering who I may be sharing the airwaves with. At about 10.25 p.m. the young girl on work experience arrived to escort me into the studio. As she opened the door I got a whiff of the familiar musty smell of the place. I gave a friendly nod to the presenter and noticed two other guests. A few minutes later the 10.30 news report started and I had a moment to introduce myself. My first fellow guest was a female charity worker offering sexual health and contraception advice to teenagers. The second was the editor of a lads' magazine. As I introduced myself to him he said, 'A bit young to be a Christian aren't you?' 'Mmm — could be an interesting night ahead,' I thought.

After the news and sport, it was time for the debate to begin. The presenter turned to me first. 'Why even bother going to church? It seems to me like a dead institution.'

I replied, 'I go to church because I believe in Jesus who is very much alive. Church is a great way of building community but also encouraging one another.'

The lady jumped in, 'Encouraging people to a boring life. The church teaches a load of rules that make life dull. For a start you lot in the church all hate sex.'

'I'm not sure where you get all of your ideas from,' I said. 'Believing in Jesus is all about a relationship. Any relationship has to have rules, otherwise it's anarchy. As for sex, God gave it to us as a gift. He loves sex and Christians do too! It's just that we believe it should take place in the confines of marriage,' I added. A hush ensued, the tone was set, and the discussion went on.

Soon enough it was 11.20 p.m. and we only had ten minutes left. I felt the debate had gone quite well. Then a telephone caller to the show really disrupted things. After exchanging pleasantries with the presenter the gentleman at the end of the phone spoke up, 'I've been living in a monogamous relationship for twelve years. My partner and I are very much in love and have a committed and honest relationship. We are good moral role models, yet the church hates us for being gay. Why is the church so homophobic? Why does the church hate gays so much?' I thought I'd managed to escape many of the most controversial phone-in questions that evening but I was clearly wrong.

I took a deep breath and started my response. 'We don't have time to discuss this in full but I do believe that God always intended sexual relationships to be purely between men and women in committed Christian marriage. He set the tone for this right from the beginning of the Bible in Genesis chapter two – when God created man he then created woman as his partner. However, I agree with you that the church can be homophobic. We can seem to make homosexuality the worst of sins and yet argue that God has no hierarchy of sin. The Bible only refers to homosexuality seven times, four in the Old Testament and three in the New. Issues such as pride and coveting are mentioned much more, but some Christians can easily seem obsessed with homosexuality.'

I continued, 'Christians speak of a Jesus who hung around with all kinds of social outcasts, yet we can make the homosexual community feel like outcasts from the church. I believe that the church has to reach out to more people in love and help individuals such as this gentleman feel like they can interact with it.' With that the presenter went to the news and sport and we were finished.

As we left the studio the editor of the lads' magazine came up to me and said, 'fair play. You argued your case well. I usually believe the church has no relevance to post-modern society whatsoever but you've made me question that. I genuinely thought that the church was only for old people yet you've shown me otherwise. You never know – in fifty years time it might still be here after all.'

His comments made me reflect deeply. The church is seen in such a bad light. Whether we like it or not, we come across as so irrelevant.

We talk of the greatest revolutionary of all time who walked the planet giving food to the hungry (John 6), sight to the blind (John 9) and life to the dead (John 11), and yet too often all that our world sees is old buildings, vicars wearing dresses, pastors who ignore current realities, and caveman beliefs unthinkingly adopted by the majority of the faithful.

A Distorted View?

I am regularly confronted with people in the world who hold the wrong view of the church. Historically Christianity has consistently had a huge impact on the Western world. Monarchs, politicians, key historical figures and entire nations themselves have seen the church and its message of hope as intrinsic to their basic make-up. How things have dramatically changed in recent times. In the West the influence of the church within society, politics and morality has been diminishing year on year for decades. So much so that what we see today can look like an increasingly amoral, secular society with no god other than self-satisfied consumerism.

As a church we can be perceived as completely detached from the real world: a gaggle of crazy, deluded, happy-clappy weirdos with nothing in common with normal people. Even the polite simply write us off as too unconventional or unorthodox to be taken seriously. As the British comedian Frank Skinner puts it in his autobiography:

> I tell you, in a society where all manner of once smirked-upon behaviour like wearing crystals and Feng Shui has become acceptable, only Christian belief can definitely guarantee you the label 'weird'.[1]

How can other such things be seen as mainstream and yet the church be perceived as weird? This has created such a cultural paradox. Truth is seen as false, the bizarre as normal, and reality as fraud. What a dramatic and disastrous change that has taken place throughout Western society! Yet many Christians have failed to even notice it happening.

Having looked at the kind of gospel that we need to proclaim to reach our world, it is good to take time in order to ask why we are currently failing to capture much ground today. As this book covers two perspectives (UK and USA), it is perhaps appropriate to concentrate on the 'worst case scenario' and in this instance that is certainly Britain!

Younger generations have always struggled with religious institutions, so it is no great surprise that today's young people seem to particularly struggle to engage with church. The bride of Christ is often seen as having little or no relevance to their lives at all except perhaps for two days: their wedding and their funeral. This has resulted in a dearth of students and young adults in the church. Therefore, many people like myself can find themselves feeling lonely and isolated within the Christian community. This has to stop, and now!

I have very few peers in the Christian community. None of my friends that I grew up with seem all that interested. As an itinerant speaker I go to forty or fifty churches a year and can spot the university towns straight away – the pews actually have young adults seated in them. If there is no university then more often than not there are no young people. It's a very difficult situation and if the decline continues then it will only be a generation or two until the church is talked of in the past tense in Britain. The situation is pretty bleak, and it requires a new passionate commitment among God's people today if anything is going to change.

Things have not always been so bad. There was a time not so long ago when Christianity formed the foundation of British society, and provided a moral compass. Its presence within the community provided stability, reassurance and a sense of direction. Going to church on a Sunday was seen as important, beneficial and edifying to both the individual and the wider community. The church school was a good place to educate your children, and Sunday school would provide the next generation with a well-rounded and wholesome worldview. Stories such as Jonah being swallowed by a great fish (Jonah 1), the walls of Jericho falling down (Joshua 6) and Paul being blinded on the road to Damascus (Acts 9), were well known and accepted. Today such stories seem little more than myth and the name of Jesus is just a swear word.

Many may argue that such days were a lifetime ago, and that this is all over the top Christian hyperbole, but that simply isn't the case. It's only been a generation or two since church buildings were used for housing worshipping congregations (in fact, in the USA, little has changed, although the cracks are beginning to appear). Today in Britain old churches can often be seen functioning as carpet warehouses, flash wine bars and squatter communities. The former England football (soccer) captain David Beckham was a regular attendee. He says, 'I was playing football with the cubs as well, which you could only do if you went to church on Sunday. So all the family – me, mum and dad and my sisters – made sure we were there every time without fail.'[2] Just a generation or so ago, when Beckham was a lad, there were social benefits in going to church.

It must shock my parents' and even more my grandparents' generations to see how church attendance and Sundays have changed. When I was a lad supermarkets were never open on a Sunday. Today Sunday trading is commonplace and it has developed far beyond just food shopping. People regularly spend their Sundays attending the cathedrals of consumerism and worshipping at the altar of the cash register.[3] I was stunned when on a Sunday afternoon I drove along the M1 past the Meadowhall Shopping Centre in Sheffield. The car park was absolutely rammed and it seemed a real shame that this is a normal activity for families on a Sunday. Ironically my nearest shopping centre even has two spires popping out of the top of it!

Sundays are no longer special in many other ways as well. There has always been Sunday league football but today it seems that everything is happening on a Sunday morning: community fairs, social events, children's birthday parties, charity fun runs, dance lessons, the list seems endless. There are increasing pressures pulling people away from attending church on a Sunday and children are growing up in a world where Sunday services are unusual. We need to ask why the church culture has disappeared in Europe, and how long it can survive in America.

For many hundreds of years, the church in Britain was the very epicentre of the community. Every town and village had a church and a school. Whether we like it or not, the church no longer holds the same position in any society outside of the USA. Today it has certainly lost this place in the UK and, if anything, has been usurped by the school and education. The former British Schools Minister David Miliband made the point some years ago that the school had to fill the void left by the church at the very heart of our communities. The fundamental problem is that the church no longer attracts people as it used to do. There simply aren't as many people going through the doors on a Sunday as there were.

In addition the church can often be perceived as outdated and is regularly accused of things that society sees as prejudiced or inappropriate. We've all heard the regular jibes in both the UK and the USA – that the church is hypocritical, homophobic and anti-sex. This is all nonsense, of course, and as churches we need to work out a strong apologetic in response to such rhetoric. 'Truth will out', as the saying goes, but it does have to be proclaimed first.

We have to be brave enough to admit that currently we simply aren't cutting it. In England, 72 per cent of people may claim to be Christian[4] yet only 6.3 per cent have a faith that's real and active enough to mean that they bother going anywhere near a church.[5] In America things look so much better, but even there the trend is consistently downward.

I was part of one of the early 'youth congregations' (or Gen X churches in America). We would meet in an alternative room with uplighters, lava lamps and tie-dyed sheets, and in the main we had a good time. However, on a purely entertainment level these places could never compete with the world. A church has no hope in the entertainment stakes against a sports event or rock concert. Without wanting to simplify things too much, this cultural shift played a huge part in many of my generation leaving the church. The total figure has been quoted as being one thousand young people per week in the UK throughout the 1990s.[6] In this Christian culture I would regularly hear others saying 'I didn't get much out of the worship today' yet inside just thought to myself 'I didn't realise it was for you!' There were a number of other reasons but many of my generation left the church simply because something more entertaining came along.

A New Hope?

I find it encouraging that in the last six or seven years much of the church's culture has changed. We have realised the need to give people an experience, and that empowering them for action is far more important than pithy entertainment. We have acknowledged that a young person (or any person in fact) needs to take a level of ownership of their faith. So much of this can be done through 'doing' as opposed to 'watching'. This change in culture has led to wonderful events such as Festival Manchester, Soul in the City, the Noise Project and NE1; allowing teenagers to serve a community and share their faith all at the same time. We call these word and deed missions, and they have led people to a greater sense of ownership of their faith. This bodes well for the future. It means that your average Christian sixteen-year-old will not debate which is more important: evangelism or social action. They see the two as entirely interlinked. You paint someone's fence to tell him or her about Jesus or you paint it to endorse the message that you've already shared. This is an incredibly positive move forward for the Christian community.

In the USA the 'emergent' church movement has resulted in the planting of new congregations and churches that are not irrelevant to contemporary generations – as 12,000 attendees at Mars Hill in Grand Rapids under the teaching of Rob Bell vividly illustrate. In Britain, too, this is helping, as many younger people are engaging with clear biblical teaching through Rob Bell's outstanding series of Nooma DVDs.

When I think about the Western church, and how it appears to be at the moment, I find myself pulled in two directions. On the one hand it's a struggle being in the corporate church with so many attractions in the world and so few people of my own age. But on the other I have so much hope and am excited for the church's future. Through my work with Youth for Christ I have seen so many young people all over Britain, and in parts of America, who are enthused about Jesus. There are many wanting to start a revolution and do things that my generation would never have dreamed possible. A new breed of teenagers has been empowered to try and change their town, community or school. This is so much more exciting than being a consumer simply sat in church and waiting to be entertained.

Amidst my excitement is an apprehension about older people's views of the young. I've seen too many enthusiastic teenagers desperate to change the world, suddenly crushed because they are told to wait until they are older, get back to reality and understand that life is not that simple. The Bible gives us the opposite message: Elisha was the youngest of twelve, Jeremiah was a youth, and many of the disciples were teenagers. I beg pastors, parents and adults to give young people a chance to change their environment. Please don't curb their enthusiasm with perceived worldly wisdom. We believe in a God who changes all the rules and gives opportunities to the least likely, a God who started his earthly ministry at the lowest point on earth, the Jordan Valley (John 1), and a God who takes the lowest and makes them the highest. Please let's not wait for them to get older, let's release and empower young people now!

The problem is that we seem to assume that we should work chronologically. Being older doesn't mean knowing better. Sometimes we need younger people to shake up the status quo. Most concerning of all is that we often seem to assume that young means bad. There was an article in the British newspaper *The Times* that looked at the way that teenagers are perceived during the school holidays:

> It is a curious view of the world that sees in groups of children (and young people) not a fund of pleasure and hope for the future, but a source of alarm and distress to local communities.[7]

Negative media coverage and the unfortunate behaviour of a small minority of young people have led to many adults often assuming the worst about teenagers. We need to move away from immediately seeing three teenagers in a park as a threat. We must have change so that when young people come into church older folk needn't be afraid. It truly is a curious view of the world that sees young people as an instant cause of alarm and distress. This is particularly true in such an otherwise politically correct environment. It always puzzles me that in such a politically correct society there are only two groups of people that you can say whatever you like about, Christians and young people.

Yes, there are problems with teenagers but no one seems to be giving them a helping hand – in fact we seem to be constantly trying to knock them down instead. I am forever hearing people having a go at the young. The British justice system is throwing ASBOs (anti-social behaviour orders) at young people as if they were confetti; the media vilify youths in hooded tops as a generation of muggers; society seems to assume that young people are constantly looking for trouble and the police treat the young as guilty until proven innocent. It is harder than ever to be a young person today.

There is so much pressure to look right, sound right and act right. Our increasingly powerful media set the pattern. Waif-like celebrities become role models to a new generation of young girls and then we wonder why eating disorders have become commonplace amongst them. Drug-abusing rock stars are all over our televisions, billboards, magazines and newspapers and we wonder why young people want to take drugs. We aren't helping them. We have more young people than ever before attempting suicide, self-harming and becoming depressed. When will we realise that they aren't completely bad and they desperately need our love? Many are learning to survive without the love and support of two parents and in a world where they are constantly crushed. If you tell someone that they're no good enough times, then they will inevitably begin to believe it.

Meanwhile 'across the pond', often even fewer opportunities are made available to the young. My dad, who is the minister of a church in Connecticut, has two elders who are thirty, and a couple of pastors the same age. But that is rare, and with respect, thirty is not all that young. So often younger workers concentrate solely on young people – and how much elder Christians can miss out. The temptation then comes to emphasise the need to change the church rather than to reach the world. Now both will usually be necessary. But shifting the deckchairs on the Titanic can never be as important as trying to save the ship, or seeking to prevent it hitting an iceberg! Young people are not the church of tomorrow but of today, and we need to make them our prime focus.

Just when you start to think, 'Wow – what an opportunity for the church to show our young people love like they have never known', you find that stories are rife about young people being thrown out of church for the most trivial of things: wearing a baseball cap, having a tattoo or piercing, playing football in the car park. The reasons are embarrassing and the regularity of such stories even more so. We have a church that, as on the radio phone-in, is seen as homophobic, a church that is felt to be irrelevant, a church that is no longer a strong moral compass to society, and a church that is perceived as finished and yesterday's thing.

What can we do to reverse this image? What can we change so that future generations view us differently, knowing the church is a place that can and will embrace them with a love that will change their lives forever? For the sake of the church and the validity of the gospel, we must do something.

Notes

1. F. Skinner, *Frank Skinner* (London, Arrow Books, 2001) p. 96
2. D. Beckham, *My Side* (London, HarperCollinsWillow, 2003) p. 23
3. R. Frost, *Freedom Fighters* (Milton Keynes, Authentic Media, 2005) p. 89
4. 2001 Census, Key Statistics for Local Authorities in England & Wales, Table KS07.
5. The English Church Census (London, Christian Research Association, 2005)
6. H. Wright, *A Workbook on Reaching and Keeping Teenagers* (London, Christian Research Association, 2002)
7. Article by Jane Shilling, *The Times* (August 3rd 2006) p. 8

SECTION TWO

From a Different Perspective

CHAPTER FOUR

Can God Change Me –
and Them? (Clive)

The Enlightenment of the eighteenth century had convinced humankind that we had
now come of age. We could work things out for ourselves.
Consequently, God could largely be laid aside and forgotten, while humans looked to themselves as the source of all
knowledge and the only true reality in life.

What was the result? In the twentieth century, the threat
of the nuclear bomb fostered a profound sense of fear that
if we ourselves were the sum total of life, we would probably mess it up. As society grew increasingly secular, we
adopted a philosophy of life that largely cut out God, and
therefore condemned the church to a permanent place on
the sidelines. The churches were largely emptied, intellec-
tuals rejected faith for humanism, and young people
rebelled with a unique intensity.

Sadly, this is still the case today. Throughout the sixties
and seventies, Christianity continued to lose much of its
remaining intellectual credibility. A population, no longer
even nominally Christian, replaced the faith of a nation with
a militant atheism or an indifferent agnosticism – or both!
Only a remnant survived.

Into this graveyard of shattered ideals blew that wind of
confusion and restlessness which marked the 1980s and
1990s. No longer could people see clear destinations and
objectives; the result both locally and nationally was an
aimless wandering. In the turmoil of financial insecurity,
ethnic confrontation, industrial unrest, problems of law and

order, and an uncertain future, the only answer appeared to be the old one, 'Let's live for today, tomorrow we die.'

Are you wondering why the brief history lesson? The answer is summarised in the words of Steve Turner's short, but brilliant poem.

> History repeats itself.
> Has to.
> No-one listens.[1]

Now in a new millennium, our self-centred, sin-sick, materialistic society still knows that it is sick, but has forgotten the cure. The result is emptiness and a deep sense of cosmic loneliness.

The Swiss psychologist Paul Tournier summarised the situation in this way:

> What is the meaning of this nostalgia for perfection which some admit and others hide, but which is inevitably there in every man and woman! It is our homesickness for Paradise...the whole of humanity suffers from what we might call the 'Paradise Lost' complex. To a world which was made as the garden for men to walk and talk with their creator God came rebellion, rejection and expulsion — since then mankind has groped through the shadow of homesickness searching for a home.[2]

The situation is further aggravated by a world which refuses to stand still for a moment, even to catch its breath. This restlessness is reflected in the way that half the population of the United States move house every year. On our own doorstep, marriages are broken as quickly and easily as they are made. Everything is in a state of flux. Nothing is static.

Everything is in turmoil. No one seems to have any answers left. And no one knows the way home.

Don't Just Sit There

They say that the apple does not fall far from the tree. I guess that Gavin and I would have to say that is right. He met Jesus having slept off the after-effects of his eighteenth pint of beer. For me, I turned briefly to 'wine, women and song' once I found that I could not change the world, and back in the sixties, I really wanted to.

Those were the days when, while other creeds brought hope for the future, Christianity seemed to offer only respectability to the present. In some regions of the world, Christianity had become synonymous with a grim, unconcerned and irrelevant selfishness, while socialism offered real potential for changing our world. I remember joining my voice with thousands of other protesters fervently chanting 'Viva Che, Viva Che, Guevara lives, Guevara lives', in honour of the great Bolivian revolutionary hero — who was already dead.

We wanted things to change for the poor, the marginalised and the oppressed; we screamed out for things to be different. I realised this desire might involve personal cost. I might need a more committed and sacrificial way of living. I needed a faith, or a philosophy of life to help me to live that way, but I (and most of my contemporaries) could not see that kind of radical lifestyle coming from Christianity.

All Christianity seemed to offer was membership in a club, and not a terribly exciting one at that. Instead of working to promote a dynamic renewal within society, the church appeared only to want to preserve the status quo. Heaven was viewed as the elixir for all pains and disappointments here on earth. In addition, participation in an exclusive, often oppressive subculture was designed to guarantee that few Christians would ever stray far from what was expected of them.

That kind of smug, insular, self-satisfied, safety-first faith could surely never help. The story is related that a Viet Cong guerilla officer said to a missionary in Vietnam, 'I would gladly die if I could advance the cause of communism one more mile... You know, as you have read to me from the Bible, I have come to believe that – you Christians have a greater message than that of communism. But I believe that we are going to win the world, for Christianity means something to you, but communism means everything to us.'[3]

Doesn't that revelation remind you of something? Isn't it just like that kind of passionate, disciplined, sacrificial commitment which Jesus preached? Isn't that zeal really the lost message of Jesus?

More Than Words Can Say

My first problem lay in my ideals. I could try to change life for others, but I couldn't change myself. To this day, I am nervous about people who can talk about an issue or a dream as if that was all that was required. Words are cheap, and often inadequate.

One day, to my great surprise, I found myself listening to the preacher. The man in question, Roger Forster, was one of the most articulate and gifted Christian communicators in Britain. I felt that if I had to sit and endure yet another evangelist droning on about a faith I could not bring myself to believe in, then I could do far worse than listen to this one. There was one drawback: Roger was an old friend of my family, and I had once boasted to him at a meal table that I was an atheist!

That statement could have been stretching the truth a little, although God certainly no longer featured in my life-plans.

I listened to this brilliant preacher, and then I rose from my chair and prepared to leave. Frankly, by this time in my life, words were not enough. But Roger stopped me in the doorway and insisted upon having a conversation. In the past, I had only talked to him about myself; I had never bothered to listen to his story. After all, a Christian could surely have little to offer a streetwise social activist.

I soon found myself to be sadly wrong. He genuinely wanted to practice what he preached. His message boiled down to a straightforward instruction — 'You need the presence and power of God in your life, because if you are going to live in God's world, then you have got to live in it God's way.'

I found that I could escape his words, but not the impact of his life. Roger's life was far from attending endless rounds of church committees and addressing geriatric congregations. He, his wife Faith, and their young family lived in London, in a house situated down by the River Thames. They opened their home to any homeless person, drug addict, or alcoholic, putting them in ex-army beds that they stacked three high on opposite sides of the guest room. There was a place for anyone who wanted a bed for the night, plus food, and it came free of charge!

Here, for the first time, I encountered a Christian who did what I believed Jesus would do. Despite all my prejudice against the church, and a very cynical and jaundiced attitude towards Christians, I had met someone who acted out the reality that I had only verbalised. This man lived it.

Before I could stop myself, I had asked the fatal question

about his motivation. No sooner than I blurted out the enquiry, 'What have you got?' I realised that I already knew the answer.

'Jesus,' came Roger's simple reply.

Two weeks later, as I walked the streets of London's East End, I finally capitulated and surrendered my life to Jesus Christ. Yes, I was still confused, and very uncertain – but something began when I prayed my hesitant prayer, 'Lord, I don't even know if you are there, but if you are, would you forgive me, and start to change my life?'

Setting out on a relationship with Jesus was the single most significant moment of my life. Many of us are not good at conceding that we have been wrong, especially when what we least wanted to be correct turned out to be exactly right all the time. I was one of those!

Furthermore, I quickly realised that my problems were far from over. In the first place, I still had church to cope with. Even if Jesus was right, surely the same could not be said of the church. The vibrant Christian life of one individual might have provided the means by which God brought me to faith, but how was he to help me overcome my deep-rooted antipathy toward the institution that bore his name?

With a Church Like This...

For all who struggle with church rather than Jesus, we definitely need to say that you are not alone.

Our modern world has clearly run out of answers to the questions that many are asking. What are we, as the church of Jesus Christ, actually doing about it? An often lonely, confused, erratic, spontaneous, lost and troubled world has shouted out for standards, for answers to how life could be different. So often the church is silent, while extreme cults have seized the opportunity to lead men further into false-hood. Meanwhile, those of us who claim to have the light of the truth revealed by Jesus too often hide in a corner of an ecclesiastical building cloaked by our own indifference. Thus, men and women are condemned to continue to walk in darkness.

We need to face up to this question: Should we blame those without the light for living in darkness, or blame those who claim to have the light for not shining?

Many are content to read books like *The Prayer of Jabez* with bated breath, anticipating all the blessings that our God might have in store for them. Actually, there is nothing intrinsically wrong with books like that. However, is Christianity only about how to keep ourselves pure and away from the world? Is it only about the blessings we can receive? Or is there something more?

Is our faith about what we get, or is it about what we can give — especially in the light of all that our God has given to us? King David expressed it succinctly when he said to the Lord, 'Who am I, and who are my people, that we should be able to give as generously as this? Everything comes from you, and we have given you only what comes from your hand' (1 Chronicles 29:14).

This verse is a salutary reminder in our dominantly 'me'-centred society that Christianity is not ultimately about us — it is about the living God. He is not satisfied with wanting people to join our nice friendly club. He is seeking people who will make his kingdom their priority, instead of their own concerns (Matthew 6:33). Then they will receive from his good hand of love all he wants to give. Jesus requires a people who want him to change their world, and they must be ready for him to use them to accomplish it. They are content to know that the rewards will come later.

Archbishop William Temple once declared that, 'The

church of Jesus Christ is the only society on earth that exists entirely for the benefit of its non-members.' He was right. The Lord Jesus always intended self-sacrifice to be the order of our lives. He died to redeem us, not to an existence of selfish ease, but to a life of selfless service. This total commitment is an inescapable part of the message of Jesus. He did not only come to save us so that we might be happy in knowing and loving him. Of course that is true, but it is only a part of the story. The purpose of his life and death was also that we might be usable servants of his kingdom.

Surprisingly enough, true happiness lies in selfless service. When Jesus outlined the 'beautiful attitudes', or qualities of godly living, in the Sermon on the Mount, he prefaced each one with the single word 'blessed'. This word does not refer to possessing advanced holiness, or to drifting through life with an angelic grin on our faces dispensing spiritual goodness. Its root meaning is simply 'happy'. When we live life in the ways outlined in the Beatitudes, we find the pathway to true happiness. Of course, this lifestyle is precisely the opposite of what our world would expect, but it is the real doorway to contentment and fulfilment. It *is* divinely possible to be both happy and holy.

Interestingly enough, the 'Jesus way' also results in spiritual promotion. On two separate occasions Jesus pointed out that the route to becoming great in God's kingdom is to first learn what it means to be the servant of all (Mark 9:35, 10:43). A life of godly service is the guarantee of joy, both now and later.

Many would affirm that the current church is in grave danger of missing out on a golden opportunity. In recent years the campaigns of evangelists like Billy Graham and Luis Palau, and the marvellous developments in local evangelism under the 'Alpha' programme, plus the work of Youth for Christ among young people, and hundreds of other significant outreaches in local churches, all testify to an enormous spiritual hunger among people today. Yet numbers are diminishing, and for the majority of people, the name of Jesus constitutes little more than a casual expletive.

Could the real problem lie, not in structures and institutions, but simply with you and me?

Kondwani, the twenty-four-year-old deputy Youth Officer for World Relief in Malawi, possessed a rather low view of the average politician. He commented that at school they had been taught that the government was not an abstract concept, while the church certainly was.

Now as a Christian, he had started to look at things a little differently. He could not see government ever changing his country. Instead, he could envision a band of brothers and sisters who had totally surrendered their lives to Jesus, who had abandoned plans for their own fulfilment, who were ready to serve others through the Spirit of Jesus, and who could pray and reach out to their contemporaries with the love of God. Suddenly it was the government that seemed like an abstract concept.

Our regret will be eternal if, by our tragic neglect, we will fail to reach our lost generation with the love of Jesus. Just because we want to have a safe and easy life, we could miss out on one of the greatest adventures available to humankind: that of changing our world for Jesus.

Notes

1. Steve Turnor, *Nice & Nasty* (London, Marchall, Morgan & Scott Ltd., 1980) p. 27
2. P. Tournier, *A Place for You* (London, SCM Press, 1968)
3. Leighton Ford, *The Christian Persuader*

CHAPTER FIVE

The Way That It Should Be (Gavin)

In the thirteen years of his life, Jake's difficult background has taught him to fight his way through each day. His dad walked out on his mum when he was only a few weeks old, leaving her to get by on what benefits the social services were prepared to offer — and they were few. His box room on the eighteenth floor of the filthy, towering council flats may not look like much, but Jake calls it home. When he was ten a local church youth worker called Alan moved onto his estate and began a lifestyle of relational evangelistic youth work. At first Jake was highly suspicious of this member of 'the God squad'. He couldn't understand why a middle-class man from the nice side of town would come and live there out of choice.

Jake and his friends made life as hard as possible for Alan. They spat in his face, slashed the tyres on his dilapidated Ford Capri, and did anything they could think of to discredit his endeavours. Despite their best efforts there was no displacing Alan. He felt a clear calling from God to be in that place so he bravely persevered in his difficult surroundings. Even so, after the best part of three years serving on the estate Alan began to feel a little disillusioned about whether or not it was all worth it. Why would God have brought him here only for nothing to happen and for him to feel entirely hopeless? Thankfully by God's grace he was about to see some reward for his tireless efforts.

On a cold winter night he sat with Jake on a rickety, graffiti-stained bench sharing his Thermos flask of tea. Despite the falling temperature and rising wind, the pair of them talked for over two hours about Jesus. At the end of the conversation Alan had the privilege of witnessing Jake coming to the point of surrendering his life to the King of kings. This was more than Alan had dreamed possible. After three years of battling against the odds, here was one of the estate ringleaders surrendering his life to Jesus. That night for the first time in over twenty years Alan was so excited that he didn't get a wink of sleep.

In the weeks that followed, Jake started out on the adventure of being a Christian. As Alan discipled him he knew that he was being transformed. He was being kinder to those around him, and felt a greater sense of meaning, worth and destiny. Jake started to see the folly of his previous ways as the chip on his shoulder became non-existent. He also began praying, reading the Bible and going to church. Having always assumed that church was boring, Jake was pleasantly surprised to find that he actually quite enjoyed it. However, he did find it hard that he was just about the only teenager there. After he had been going to the church every Sunday for about nine months, his minister preached on baptism and offered individuals the opportunity to be baptised (as Jesus himself had been). Jake knew straight away that this was for him. The minute the service was over, he headed straight for the minister. Together they agreed that Jake should be baptised.

Jake went to the worst school of hard knocks in the area – an inner-city all boys comprehensive. He bravely invited his entire form group of thirty to his baptismal service. Amazingly about twenty or so of them agreed. He told them to get to the church in good time, sit on the back rows and, 'Be patient with the old people at church. They aren't used to young people and may not know how to relate to you.'

When the day of the baptism finally came, people began filling up the church. The adults arriving at the church were somewhat stunned and intimidated by the rough-looking lads sat on the back couple of rows. After all Jake was the only young person at the church. The regular church attendees tried to conceal quite how uncomfortable they were feeling. Their efforts were in vain as it was perfectly clear to anyone in the building that the women were terrified. The men tried to act cool but it was obvious that their hands were firmly in their pockets clinging tightly to mobile phones, car keys and wallets. That Sunday morning there were no men to be seen raising their arms during worship!

Eventually the time came for Jake to give his testimony. 'You may have noticed something different this morning. Unlike the rest of you here I have actually invited some people to come to church that don't yet know Jesus.' This comment from the plucky young lad at the front caused corporate shock throughout the congregation. Alan, however, sat there with the widest possible smile feeling incredibly proud of Jake and blown away by the God who's in the business of changing lives. Jake continued: 'I've told them to make a decision about Christianity based on how you treat them after the service.' This time a nervous laughter swept through the congregation. These young lads at the back were not the church type. Not one member of the regular congregation had any desire to go anywhere near them.

When the baptisms were over the scenes that followed were quite remarkable. Through a mixture of guilt and obligation the adults began to gather around the young lads like a swarm of bees. These now poor, defenceless young lads each had ten to fifteen adults surrounding them and offering them more and more cups of tea. For one day only the church could have done with some emergency portaloos!

What It All Means

The story of Jake is a wonderful one. Here is a young man who truly lives out what it means to be a Christian. He is part of the local Christian community, yet also inhabits the real world (Matthew 5:13–16). He enjoys worshipping at church but is also keen to spread the gospel message (Romans 1:15). He loves his Christian family yet is unafraid to challenge them (1 Corinthians 14:36). I dream of a whole church that is one day full of Jake-type characters of all ages, shapes and sizes. We as a church need to raise our game. At the moment we simply aren't cutting it in terms of evangelism. We need to focus our efforts and reach out to the world in love (Matthew 19:19).

Moving the furniture, redesigning the programme, and entertaining the children are all good and right, but not in place of reaching our world. Young people are vitally important to the church's future. If we want to change the world then our Western efforts need to be largely refocused on the young. After all, 75 per cent of those who become Christians do so under the age of twenty.[1] I've heard it quoted regularly that this can become as high as 85 per cent by the age of twenty-three. This should radically effect how a church operates. I've tested the statistic in many churches by asking people to put their hands up if they came to Jesus under the age of twenty. Nearly every hand goes up! Therefore if we want to have a vibrant, growing church then we need to invest in the young. I wonder whether or not your church invests 75–85 per cent of its resources into young people, as this would seem the logical correlation in terms of missionary activity! Furthermore, recent US studies show that the vast majority become Christians through personal contact and relationship. Teaching and training our own young Christians to germinate rather than just survive is an absolutely vital priority on both sides of the Atlantic.

For the majority of young people today you never know what's waiting just around the corner. The fact is that difficult and disengaging teenagers of today could, with the right investment, go on to be tomorrow's Christian heroes. It's interesting to look through the pages of church history and see the ages at which many of our leaders came to faith: Charles Spurgeon (15), George Whitefield (16), William Booth (15), C. T. Studd (16), James Hudson Taylor (15), D. L. Moody (18), Amy Carmichael (15) and Billy Graham (17).[2] I'm deeply excited at the prospect of some of these Christians being reached and raised up today. However, if this is to happen then significant change is required, and quickly.

In the Sermon on the Mount we are called as a body of Christians to be salt and light within the world and then 'a city on a hill that can't be hidden' (Matthew 5:13, 14), yet so often we hide ourselves from the world. The famous theologian Dietrich Bonhoeffer wrote about what it truly means to be the salt of the earth:

> Up to now we must have had the impression that the blessed ones were too good for this world, and only fit to live in heaven. But now Jesus calls them the salt of the earth – salt, the most indispensable necessity of life. The disciples, that is to say, are the highest good, the supreme value which the earth possesses, for without them it cannot live.[3]

As the people of God we must be this salt. We are not too good for the world; we are just the seasoning for it. I meet so many Christians who appear to live life being superior, and never vulnerable. They talk of the 'lost' as if they are nothing. We need to remember that we are simply hopeless people who've found great hope in Jesus and the lost, those still outside of Christ, need this hope too. We must be amongst the world, as without us it cannot live!

On Whose Terms?

In principle many of us are happy to be salt and light so long as it's on our terms, in our church building, and within our comfort zone. When Jesus makes Peter the rock on which he will build his church it is made plainly obvious that the church is about people and not bricks and mortar (Matthew 16:18). However, we can often set a different agenda for ourselves, by subconsciously valuing the role of church within its four walls more highly than its mission to the community. We need to value people who can interact in the real world. I know I share the struggle of preferring to spend time with those who don't know Jesus in an evangelistic sense, over going to three church meetings during the week.

Yet, this can be really hard. We can be perceived as less than committed to the cause – we may be viewed as unfaithful – for not coming to everything the church does. And yet we are called to share Jesus with a hurting world. I'd rather be accused of backsliding by my fellow-Christians now than face the gaze of Jesus in heaven as he reviews my failure to share his love on earth.

Our Western church claims to follow the example of Jesus. If we mean this, then for many of us change is required. Jesus himself spent a great deal of his ministry meeting people where they were at and engaging with everyday issues (such as farming) in order to relate to them. By contrast, we often seem to value organised church activity more highly. Our Jesus made time to speak to a woman at a well who was despised and rejected

(John 4). He made a point of engaging with a hated, tiny, cheating tax collector in a tree (Luke 19). Yet we can appear to give the greatest respect to those who are so busy attending church meetings that they haven't had a night at home in three weeks, and have never met their neighbours. Many Christians seem to be competing to see who can win the most points for going to meetings at church whilst those in the world around them are going to hell. It all seems entirely topsy-turvy.

Surely those who engage with contemporary society are exactly the evangelists a dying Western church needs. It's an incredible spiritual gift to be able to bring Jesus into the conversation within everyday scenarios. Churches should be praying for those who witness in the world – these are our missionaries. If Jesus were here today then he wouldn't be hanging around a church building going to endless meetings. His compassion for the lost would necessitate his being out there amongst the people. Let us not forget that the Son of God started his public ministry not at a great religious festival but on the third day of a week-long wedding where the wine had run out (John 2).

The Jesus Way

A God who hung out with lepers, prostitutes and tax collectors is hardly going to choose to spend all his time amongst middle-class church attendees. He would be far more likely to hang around with those whom no one loves. It's important to ask ourselves: who are the people in our towns that nobody loves? Perhaps the answer to this question should dictate the next outreach programme for your church. It is we who should be standing by these folk and helping them come one step closer to knowing Jesus.

Jesus was such a radical and yet we often appear to have

created a faith that can be seen as watered down and having lost its edge. We have the potential to be so safe that it's doubtful anyone feels all that threatened. All over the developing world, governments are terrified of the church and the effect, power and influence it has. I've stood in Sudan where the church is perceived as such a threat that the northern operation based out of the capital city, Khartoum, simply has to see it destroyed. All over the developing world the church is seen as highly dangerous.

One read of the hugely popular and moving *Heavenly Man* by Brother Yun proves the point again. In China the authorities feel that they must kill off the church. Powers all over the planet are terrified of the church and totally determined to get rid of it. Yet all this persecution seems to make no difference. If anything the church becomes stronger amidst the pain. The blood of martyrs fertilises the ground for the church to grow. And this happens time and again. Paradoxically in the West we have adopted a strand of Christianity that rarely threatens to disrupt the status quo. Even though we are following the most uncompromising revolutionary ever, somehow we seem to dilute his message and even try to make it appear mundane. We can be so far removed from his example that if Jesus visited us here on earth today he might well be far too radical and find himself unwelcome or vilified in a number of our churches!

The Western church should value mission that takes place in informal settings and relationships. Jesus used everyday meetings with people, and often in one-on-one situations to share his message. One good example is found in John 3 when Nicodemus comes to secretly meet Jesus during the night. There was no pomp and ceremony and no great religious festival, just a private encounter and a conversation. We must seek to encourage and develop a church in which one of the most important things we do is sharing the Lord in love through our everyday lives. When did you last hear a sermon on sharing your faith at work? Or communicating Jesus in the supermarket? Or witnessing over a pint of beer in a pub? Or a coffee in Starbucks? These are exactly the kind of situations that the church needs to be addressing and encouraging. We need to mobilise our people into action. We must take seriously our links to the world. We have to reach out to others. We are compelled to be amongst those who no one else loves. Why? Because that is where our Jesus would be.

The question 'If you were put on trial for being a Christian, would there be enough evidence to convict you?' has been famously asked before and remains an incredibly strong challenge today. Does the life you live show clear signs of the God you are living for? In your everyday situation, amongst those you work with, in your family home, when out in your community, when driving your car, when you haven't slept well the night before, when someone else is rude to you – in all of these situations is there evidence for you living a life for Jesus? We need to all start living in a way that is no longer confined to church and is out there amongst the people sharing the message of Jesus.

Putting on a good performance of Christianity amongst our fellow Christians is not enough – we need to do our utmost to live for Jesus all the time. Yes, we'll make mistakes, but his grace is sufficient for us (2 Corinthians 12:9), and we have the fantastic promise that he is with us always (Matthew 28:20). In other words, Jesus requires every sinew of our being, capacity of our brain, energy in our bodies and devotion of our hearts. If we corporately did this then it wouldn't take as much as we might think to change the world.

If every Christian in the West helped one person a week to find faith, it would take just one month for the whole of

Britain and the USA to become Christian. This is both surprising and encouraging. If we can help everyone to share their faith, then the West could follow parts of Asia, Latin America and Africa in falling on its knees before the King of kings.

I'm certain that there would be enough evidence to convict Jake of being a Christian: he's an example to us all. But we need a church where there is enough evidence to convict every last one of us. This way we could change our communities, workplaces and schools. We could see the church back at the heart of the community. We would be more dangerous and the world could no longer ignore us and think nothing of our mission. Surely the future has to look like this – the alternative is terrifying. The only other option is that we stay locked away, hiding our light, rather than rescuing the 94 per cent in the UK, or the ever increasing amount in the USA, who never go near church!

Notes

1. P. Brierley, *Reaching & Keeping Teenagers* (Tumbridge Wells, Monarch, 1993)
2. G. Calver, *Disappointed with Jesus?* (Oxford, Monarch Books, 2004) p. 16
3. D. Bonhoeffer, *The Cost of Discipleship* (London, SCM Press Ltd., 1959) p. 104
4. 2001 Census, Key Statistics for Local Authorities in England & Wales.

CHAPTER SIX

Nothing by Halves (Gavin)

The run-up to Christmas is one of my favourite times of the year. The shops are full of brightly coloured decorations, the streets are lit up, the radio blasts out endless renditions of the same age-old Christmas anthems and the carol services and Christmas events are just around the corner.

A few years ago, about six weeks before the big day, my wife Anne and I sat down for a chat to make sure we'd got all our plans in place for the upcoming festivities. I had met my beautiful wife Anne at the London School of Theology, and we married the summer after we completed our respective degrees. Three and a half years later, things between us couldn't be better. We were the best of friends and very much in love. We appeared to have a wonderful life and in most ways that was true. We lived and worked in the Midlands for Youth for Christ, had many friends and were settled into a friendly and welcoming church.

As we began chatting about Christmas our conversation soon wandered off on an unrelated tangent. We started talking about babies. We both felt that now might be the right time to stop using contraception and start trying for a family. For the first few months we were in no great hurry. Anne's periods came and went and there was no real sense of disappointment. 'In your timing, Lord,' we kept praying, believing that it would happen some time soon. As the months rolled on the situation became increasingly difficult.

People all around us were getting pregnant, many by

accident, and yet we had this desire for a baby and no imminent sign of one arriving. Being involved in youth ministry
means that you come across many pregnant teenagers and
these seemed particularly hard to accept. It didn't seem
fair, especially because many of these young people didn't
want a child anyway. However, statistics are an interesting
thing at times like these and we clung on for comfort to the
fact that the average couple takes eight months to conceive.

By the time that the summer had come around the whole
situation was starting to become harder still. I had assumed
that Anne would be pregnant by now and we were almost
past the average conception time. I set off to speak at a conference called New Wine, and had to do some Bible teaching, counselling and leadership all geared to challenging
people to move on in God — I had a great week. Having
been speaking every day I decided to go to the workers celebration service on the Thursday afternoon. The theme for
the week had been 'Hope' and at this celebration five or six
couples gave testimony of the Lord having given them
babies after long periods of trying. What nice stories, I
thought, as I realised by now that I wanted a child more
than anything else in the world.

On returning from New Wine, Anne and I chatted and it
felt like we were both really ready for a baby now. None of
the previous calm remained. We really wanted a child and
the sooner the better. Each month we would pray about it
every day, earnestly believing that the Lord was going to
give us the baby we so desired. After all in our line of work
where everyone seemed to be getting pregnant by accident
left, right and centre, we wondered why we shouldn't when
we were so deliberately trying — and praying. Time would
drag out, and then right on cue Anne would get her period
like clockwork each month and the disappointment was
growing all the while. Every time that period came it felt

like something inside me died. The great hope that rose to a crescendo at the end of Anne's cycle was consistently crushed in an instant. And where was the God I trusted when I knew what I wanted him to do?

Life became extremely hard. At least once a week we'd get someone telling us of another woman falling pregnant. We tried to be pleased for them but it was tough, especially as everyone seemed to be getting pregnant within the first two or three months of trying.

Church was testing as well. We go to a wonderful community church but it is full of kids. Every time we went we would see the families of three and four children and wonder why we hadn't been given one. None of this was helped by the fact that all around us we were being asked when we would start a family? Did we have any children? How many children did we want? The world seemed to be full of unhelpful reminders of what we didn't have: every other woman seemed pregnant, each environment we found ourselves in filled with families, and all television adverts were for nappies. Our shared desire for children had become all-consuming.

Month after month ended in disappointment. The heartache and frustration coiled together was making the whole experience incredibly strained. Eventually we reached another Christmas. We'd been trying for a baby for over a year. We headed to America to have Christmas with my family. My parents had recently become pastors of a church and this was our first time worshipping there. It was really hard. Being kind, interested and polite people, the members of my parents' congregation wanted to get to know us. The difficulty was that everyone in the church seemed to ask us the same three questions we had always been asked in England: How long have you been married? Do you have any children? And would you like a family?

This whole situation was becoming unbearable. I just wanted to escape from the constant barrage of the world. I felt like wearing a sandwich board around me saying: 'Yes I'm married, no I don't have any children, but yes, I would like one more than anything.' Not really knowing what to do next, Anne and I stayed up one night and had a long chat with my dad about the problem. We prayed together and had a sense of peace giving the situation back to God once more. However, I was becoming increasingly frustrated with God. Why couldn't we just conceive? Dad encouraged us to go for tests, as that is what is recommended after a year of unsuccessful attempts to conceive a baby.

We decided to wait one more month, optimistically convinced that the Lord might save us the tests. But completely on time, Anne's period arrived. It was truly heartbreaking. As we looked at one another we knew what we had to do. We made an appointment.

So we came to be sitting there in the bland, cold surgery as our doctor explained all the procedures. Anne would have blood tests and I would have to give a sperm sample. If these were all clear then there would be a laborious process of gynaecological tests that Anne would have to go through. The doctor explained that these could be quite invasive and would take up to twelve months in total. I remember looking over at Anne as we sat in the doctor's surgery and feeling such compassion towards her because she might have a problem. This poor wife of mine who was so wonderful deserved better than to have a fertility issue. We went ahead and had the initial tests.

Anne's results were available after three days whilst mine would take five. Unless there was a problem the receptionist could tell you the results over the phone. Anne was so nervous and as she held the phone it shook manically in her grip. I knew that I had to help so I grabbed the handset and rang for her. I'm usually very confident but as I held the phone I could feel my whole body tensing up with anxiety. I pulled myself together and dialled the number. 'Everything is clear with your wife's tests, Mr Calver,' the receptionist politely informed me. Anne and I felt a great sense of relief. However, in the back of my mind I still felt for her, as she would have to go through the process of those long gynaecological tests.

Two days later it was my turn. Strangely I was far less nervous for myself than I had been for Anne. I confidently rang the receptionist and was somewhat surprised when she said 'You need to make an appointment with the doctor straight away, Mr Calver. In fact there is one available in fifteen minutes time if you would like it?' In shock we took the appointment and with very little time to think, arrived at the surgery in a whirlwind.

We walked gingerly into consultation room four and took a seat facing a computer screen full of statistics. The doctor was doing her level best to look hopeful, but before she said anything I saw something that made my heart sink. The computer screen was full of white text but at the top under my name was written 'sperm sample'. Alongside the white text was one red word in bold capital letters: ABNORMAL. What on earth did this mean? What was going to happen? For the first time I genuinely realised that it could actually be me that had the problem. Through this entire process I had secretly assumed that Anne was the one who was stalling things.

The doctor spoke up, 'Thanks for coming in. I'm afraid that it's not all good news. Gavin, you are not sterile but neither are you considered fertile. Your sperm have a low motility – fundamentally, they are lazy,' she said. 'What on earth does that mean?' I thought. She explained it all statistically and said that we had an outside chance of conceiving, but that equally we might never have a baby. Our chances of having one were about a third as good as a so-called 'normal couple'. Had we been thirty-five years old and not in our twenties then we would have had virtually no chance, she added. I couldn't believe what I was hearing. I had a problem. It was because of me that Anne wasn't pregnant. How could this be? Again I thought that all around me were stories of fourteen-year-olds getting pregnant, abortions and abandoned children, yet we might never have one. It all seemed so unfair.

Infertility is a reality for so many couples, but I didn't pause to ask why we should be any different to them. All we did eventually was to leave the surgery and go home. It was Friday afternoon and the whole weekend was horrible. Preaching twice on the Sunday was a particular strain. I meant every word that I proclaimed but I probably thought about it more than usual and it certainly cost me to preach of the glory of God and his bountiful provision that day.

Over the next forty-eight hours the dust settled a little. I was really hurting. Anne was great about it and reassured me that she'd rather have no children and me than not be together, but it still killed me inside. It broke my heart every time I looked at her. I knew how much she wanted a baby and yet in choosing me she might never have one. That was enough to break me. I'm very much the alpha male and just expected reproduction to happen. After all I've always fixed things, yet here was something I could do nothing about. All of a sudden I felt like half a man. Surely the most natural thing is for a man to spread his seed and if I couldn't do that then what kind of failure did that make me?

We knew we needed some help so we told a few people that were close to us as we were desperate for both prayer and support. We sat down with one particular couple. They're great people and Anne and I both get on brilliantly with each of them. As we shared they listened intently. We often do the listening in our relationships but today it was obvious that we needed to be heard. Eventually the wife spoke up, 'With all you do for Jesus, the lives you lead, the miles you travel, the sacrifices you've undertaken, has this made you question him, his goodness and existence?' Impulsively, I said, 'No way!' What a strange question, I thought to myself.

Consumers or Followers?

God is great (Titus 2:13). Just because things go wrong in our lives doesn't stop him being amazing. Just because life doesn't work out exactly how we want it to, it doesn't stop him being great. If we never had children then nothing would change; God was still good. The whole experience made me realise how important it is that our faith isn't fragile and based purely on what we receive. After all, no relationship is a healthy one if we become consumers and base its value on what we get out of it. Jesus calls us to be anything but consumers when he commands us to sacrifice everything we have and are for his purposes (Matthew 10:37–42).

Sadly it is very easy for even the most orthodox of evangelicals to let a little bit of prosperity gospel creep into their thoughts at this juncture. As Christians, health and wealth are ours by right, if God is good then nothing can go wrong! It reminds me of the classic sixth-form 'Grill a Christian' question, 'Why does a loving God allow suffering?'

'If things go wrong for us then this God can't be real' – how is that in any way a credible ideology? If Jesus had applied this to himself then how would he explain having to be born in a courtyard as the inn was full, or being left behind at the temple while his parents headed home (Luke 2)? These are the only two incidents in scripture of a pre-adult Jesus and yet in both of them as a consumer he got a raw deal. And as he grew up, things didn't exactly improve for him! If the stock market crashed tonight then the Christian stockbroker should be able to get up tomorrow morning and sing 'Great is thy faithfulness' as much as if the stock market had been fine. The greatness, existence and faithfulness of God are not dependent upon our specific individual circumstances. We are not consumers, we are followers. Jesus' challenging call of 'Follow me' contains no promises of ease or comfort.

When we become Christians we commit to follow Jesus for the rest of our lives. For me it's a bit like marriage. I was twenty-one when I stood opposite Anne and said such promises as 'for better, for worse', 'for richer, for poorer', 'in sickness and in health' and 'till death do us part.' This was followed up with the promise that 'all that I am I give to you, and all that I have I share with you'. I had no idea how the years would turn out, what challenges life would throw at us and the ways in which the enemy might try and cause discord between us. Yet I knew that I loved this girl, and that by the grace of God we'd ultimately make it work and I would stand by her. Those promises were hard to make, as I understood that for the rest of my life things would never be the same again. As long as we were both alive no decision could ever again be made selfishly, no hardship walked away from without a second thought, and life was no longer about just my contentment, as the two of us had become one (Genesis 2:24). In a similar way, my faith in Jesus must not be dependent on when things are good, when life works out, when I feel great and when it benefits me.

Some of us may need to make wedding-type promises to the King of kings. After all, when you commit to Jesus, you promise to serve him with everything. There is no room for giving up when the going gets tough. How could a fertility issue stop me believing in Jesus? For some it will and so we need to all make sure that our faith is built on stronger stuff. Like the parable Jesus tells in Matthew 7, we must make certain that we give Jesus everything and build our faith on solid rock – not sand that can be easily flattened. We need to tell Jesus that we are with him 'for better, for worse', 'for richer, for poorer', 'in sickness and in health' and till death takes us home to be with him. We could follow this up with the promise that 'All that I am I give back to you, and all that I have I share with you'.

This Christianity thing never claimed to be an easy ride. James 1 stresses quite the opposite: 'Consider it pure joy, my brothers, whenever you face trials of many kinds, because you know that the testing of your faith develops perseverance' (verses 2–3). The Christian life is tough but it's well worth it. David Field points us toward the example of Jesus: he spent most of his ministry struggling or under pressure. He had nowhere he could truly call home, he wept by his friend's tomb (John 11), he was constantly being watched and accused of breaking Pharisaical laws (Matthew 12), he felt profound compassion for his people and their needs (Matthew 9:36), he sweated with mental agony in the garden of Gethsemane (Matthew 26) and died in torment on the cross (Matthew 27). Significantly he also warned his followers that they would not escape the stresses and strains that he himself had to face (Matthew 5).[1]

We need to realise that it won't always be a nice comfortable existence. No honest Christian testimony ends with the fairy tale line, 'and they lived happily ever after'. Things will go wrong. To quote a Christian cliché: 'We live in a fallen world.' For Anne and I, as for any of us, the question is not 'Does God exist in the hard times?' but 'Are you walking closely with him through the struggle?' After all, a relationship that just finishes when it gets hard is not worth a great deal. Relationship with commitment means so much, but without our commitment, what is a Christian life worth? We need to stick with Jesus and persevere. The wonderful old *Footprints* poem puts it superbly:

> I love you and would never, never leave you. During your times of trial and suffering when you see only one set of footprints... It was then that I carried you.[2]

This Christian life is not to be done by halves. When you surrender your life to Jesus you give him everything. Where you live, who you marry, what you do. All of your life is his. You don't hold something back for yourself. It won't always be easy, but the wonderful news is that we'll never be alone!

Note

1. D. Field, *James* (Leicester, Crossway Books, 1998) p.24
2. Mary Stevenson

CHAPTER SEVEN

So What in the World is God Doing? (Clive)

Occasionally **I wonder what** it would be like to have a church beyond borders. Imagine what it would be like to be part of the vast universal church where our own petty nationalisms break down, as we learn the meaning of being one body in Christ Jesus.

This kind of unity would be such good preparation for eternity with Jesus, and with each other! For contrary to what some may hope, one day there will be no separate nations, ethnic groups, denominational factions, or cultures with their own special reserved areas of heaven where they can avoid everyone else. Jesus did not want his church to be split by culture, ethnic background, disagreements, gossip, or any other problems. The heart of Jesus has always been that his followers would be 'one' glorious and worldwide church, ready to reign with him.

What are the implications of this 'oneness'? For a start, there would be no American Christians in heaven. Neither will there be any British ones. In heaven, we will have gone beyond distinctions like African, Asian, Australian, Armenian, or any other nationality. Those distinctions will be obliterated in the glorious knowledge that we are all part of one family.

At that time, we will recognise what is involved in our desire to belong to each other, and will discover what it means to become a part of one another. We will start to realise together the meaning of being the people of God, and the bride for which King Jesus has returned.

Thus an enormous group of people is going to be drawn together out of every 'kindred, tribe, and nation'[1]. We will be called and reborn into one great family that extends worldwide – and will never end.

All One in Christ Jesus

A few years ago, this family concept might have seemed much too strange and bizarre, more the language of Star Wars than of contemporary reality. However, today the words 'global village' no longer sound like a remote fantasy. Email and the Internet reduce our ignorance and broaden our horizons to all that is happening in our world. Just what is this world like?

Let's think outside of the box for a moment. If it were possible to shrink the population of planet earth down to a small village that consisted of precisely one hundred people, and it was suddenly located in our backyard, how would it look?

First of all, fifty-one would be female and only forty-nine male, so there would be more women than men.

Only thirty would be white, the other seventy would be non-white. There would be fifty-seven Asians, twenty-one Europeans, fourteen from the Americas (North, Central, or South), and the remaining eight would be Africans.

Around thirty would be Christians, the remaining seventy drawn from all other faiths, or none.

Eighty of these people would have to live in substandard accommodations, and fifty of them would suffer from ongoing malnutrition.

One person would always be near death, while another would be approaching birth.

Only one out of a hundred people would have the privilege of a college (university) education, while seventy out of every hundred people would still be unable to read, and not one in a hundred would own a computer.[2]

Viewed in this light, we can understand why the 'have nots' will often retain a 'difficult attitude' towards those who have so much in comparison to themselves. Yet the Holy Spirit views us all part of one body. Therefore, we might as well get used to the idea while we are here on earth.

If we are to take this family concept seriously, then we will have to live up to the message that we proclaim. A watching world must be allowed to see Christ's alternative society in action. Ignorance of one another's conditions will be replaced by partnership, and indifference will be replaced by prayer. Instead of a paternalistic one-way contact from the economically powerful to the materially powerless, we will both give and receive ministry from one another.

Unfortunately, we have too often been content to be starved of information about what God is doing in countries elsewhere. Often we have allowed impersonal statistics to be our major source of information about our brothers and sisters. The time has come to listen to the stories of what God is doing in other parts of his forever family.

Meanwhile, we allow 80 per cent of the resources that the Lord Jesus produces for his entire church to be consumed by one continent, North America. While approximately 20 per cent of the need utilises 80 per cent of the available resources, 80 per cent of the need is reduced to having only 20 per cent of the material provision made available by God's people.

Behind these bland statistics lies a dramatic contrast. Church escalators, fountains and powder rooms exist in one part of the world, while brothers and sisters only five thousand miles away live without Bibles, vehicles, or the resources to provide food and medicine to their dying people.

I remember the anguish of watching Luel Akot, a young mother in Southern Sudan, laying her eighteen-month-old baby daughter on the ground to die – as we watched helplessly. I knew that in this nation people were being dramatically converted in large numbers. In fact, whole villages and communities were wonderfully coming to Christ.

Southern Sudanese congregations were becoming some of the fastest growing churches in the world. Or they would be, if only the number of conversions could keep up with the death rate.

One North American pastor, an old friend of mine, gave this distinct and salutary reminder of how he viewed the responsibilities of his congregation: 'Imagine arriving in heaven and being greeted by a Sudanese brother in Christ. How do you explain why you sat back and allowed him to die before his time? One small gift of just over fifty dollars would have given him and his family another year of life and service for Jesus – and perhaps by then the famine would have been over.'

You see, many of these deaths could have been prevented, and by me…not just by everyone else.

On the Front Line

In those countries and churches where suffering for Jesus is almost a way of life, I actually witness the greatest degree of spiritual fervency and maturity. Iran would certainly qualify as a case in point.

This nation seems to be regarded by most Americans, and a growing number of Brits, as one of the most hostile nations on earth. We view it as a place of tyranny and injustice. However, after visiting there, I don't think this is the whole truth. We may dislike the idea of being forced to admit that Iran does have – by the standards of that region of the world – both a relatively stable government and a developing society. It also has a precarious and limited measure of religious freedom.

Even more significant, no one is completely convinced about which way things will develop. Few can be confident in the course of action that the President of Iran will take. Amidst such uncertainty, the indigenous churches in Iran could be forgiven for being nervous, tentative and silent about their faith. But nothing could be further from the truth.

We never pause to imagine that the church might actually be alive and well in Iran! Nor that it might cost our brothers and sisters dearly in terms of pressure and suffering to live there as Christians. Nor can we imagine how wonderful the results might be.

While there are remnants of the ancient Armenian and Assyrian churches in Iran that have withstood the test of time, what's also exciting are the new pockets of emerging believers. There are probably more than 10,000 evangelical Christians, who meet together in over twenty-five small churches. These churches generally have to meet in private to avoid inflammatory public opinion or the interest of the secret police.

The largest of these churches would be the Assemblies of God in Teheran, which has over seven hundred people attending on a Sunday. This particular church is so fearless that it advertises its presence with a large metal cross that is attached to the front of the building – it is even raised up in the air so that no one can miss it. Recently the church leaders were interrogated in police custody for the weekend. CNN featured pictures of this church, but few viewers would have recognised the powerful witness represented by the building itself – or the believers who worship each Friday within it.

The Pentecostal Bishop of the Iranian churches confesses that he takes delight in pointing out to the secret police that they have difficulty taking any direct action against the Christian believers. He states the reason is because when they put the Christians in jail, a new constituency of different people arises to speak about the love of Jesus.

If the police close down the church, it will soon re-emerge in someone's home, because church is not a building, but a people. These Iranian believers insist that only Jesus can close down his church.[3]

There is, of course, always the ultimate deterrent. The authorities could certainly have their leaders put to death, but this would prove to be counter-productive. As the Bishop insists, the blood of the martyrs will always prove to be the seed of the church!

Before we dismiss such comments as extremism, or the vain babblings of those who would never dream of putting them into practice, I should point out that a few years ago, I had the privilege of conducting the memorial service for the Bishop's brother, who was martyred for his faith.

Don't You Know There's a War On?

Twenty-five years ago when I worked for Youth for Christ in Britain, the war on terror was far removed from the Middle East. The emphasis focused on communism, rather than Islam. In those days, a crackling radio receiver could transmit a poignant – if disjointed – message from behind the Iron Curtain: 'We are at the front. In the front line. And this front line is all around us because the enemy has surrounded us on all sides. We are surrounded by the godless. There is not a single place which is free from attack – the press, art, the theatre, schools, official institutions, everything is occupied by the godless. The laws are designed to suffocate religion. We've been at the front for a long time.'

These words came from a broadcast out of the former Soviet Union. Now decades later, our focus of attention has changed, although in many large areas of Eastern Europe, conversation about Christianity is still discouraged, and attempts are made to neutralise the church.

Christian Leadership

The fact will remain that the years of persecution in countries like Russia and China have done little long-term damage to the growth and spiritual development of the church. Once again the words of the second-century church historian, Tertullian, have proven to be correct: 'The blood of the martyrs is the seed of the church'.

Incredibly, this principle almost always seems to be the case. From the mid-point of the twentieth century onward, the unprecedented growth in what began as small house churches within China and Eastern Europe only paralleled the flood of converts in South-East Asia, Africa and Latin America.

Today, little has changed. Measured by the sheer numbers of those attending churches worldwide, Christianity is no longer primarily a Western religion.

In southeastern Africa, Christianity is alive and well, to say the least. Until 1988, the Communist regime in power had placed a ban on Christian development. However, today the church in Mozambique is arguably the fastest-growing in the world. Little of this growth can be directly attributed to the influence of Western missionaries. Undoubtedly their contributions have been somewhat helpful, but this movement has been largely African, and the momentum has come directly from the Holy Spirit.

I remember first meeting Sybil in Mozambique in 1998. Sybil is a South African missionary, and came from just across the border in South Africa. In those days, she was running just three weekly Bible clubs for around two hundred Mozambican children and young adults in an area that was hugely influenced by witchcraft. Today, many of those children have met Jesus and some are now leading Bible clubs themselves. Tens of thousands of families are larger, because their children have survived childhood, thanks in large measure to the training in health and hygiene given to mothers and children by Sybil and her fellow World Relief workers (almost all Mozambicans). Previously, vast numbers would have died before reaching five years of age.

Unsurprisingly, all this growth has produced teams of indigenous Christians that travel from village to village carrying the good news of Jesus. Many churches are being planted, and I have personally met with a number of witch doctors who have been converted. At the time of writing, Sybil's Bible clubs reach out to about 200,000 young Mozambicans each week – and she talks of the day that number will reach a half a million.

Such good news about Jesus is not always popular to the contemporary western mind, with its bias to cynicism and scepticism. Our own brand of press and media censorship has sometimes prevented ordinary people in the West from even being aware that we are living during the time of the greatest movement of God, both numerically and geographically, this world has ever seen.

Meanwhile, a calm and gentle breeze drifts across the church in the West. The casual visitor could be excused for feeling that all is largely 'business as usual'. An overwhelming commitment to generosity and compassion for brothers and sisters suffering in the face of persecution or natural disaster; a passionate enthusiasm for persistent prayer or

spontaneous worship; a sense of incredible urgency pro-
voked by the fact that millions are heading for an eternity
without Jesus; or a genuine excitement at all that the living
God is doing among his people – such phenomena are spas-
modic at best, and sadly, are rarely witnessed among most
of us!

To be sure, occasional ripples spread across the bland
surface of normal church life. Possibly an internal argument, an emergent new cult, a doctrinal over-emphasis, or
. a cash flow problem will disturb the scene for a moment or
two...but fear not, these will quickly pass away. New
organisations and initiatives will occasionally emerge, while
old ones continue in perpetuity, so we have more options to
achieve the same objective (with fresh organisational
bureaucracies needing financial support).

Sometimes, a new and vibrant evangelistic initiative will
emerge as a special effort in the life of the church, making a
fresh attempt to reach those who still live outside of Christ.
Sadly, these enterprises soon subside, and unfortunately,
internal gossip and ready criticism are quick to fill any vac-
uum they leave. Tragically, little long-term change seems to
take place. The results are only too predictable, as there is not
much evidence of genuine growth. Additionally, there is minimal impact on a population who make their own comment
on their view of our Christian credibility – with their feet.

Persecution in the West is very different than that in the
East. Rather than taking the form of overt opposition, it is
subtle and insidious. Dull apathy, empty churches, plus the
facade of respectable adherence to an institutional church,
all contribute to deny to the church a powerful role in society. Most people retain a small compartment of their lives
for what they call Christianity – but it's no more than a
word to them. They're devoid of genuine conviction.

A friend had been visiting church leaders in an Eastern

European country. At the end of his trip, one of the senior leaders paused to encourage him. He gave the normal assurance of regular prayer, but added a word of warning: 'Please tell our brothers and sisters in England that we are praying for them as well, because we know that they are not living as God wants them to!'

One morning we will wake up to the reality that a massive struggle has taken place for the tortured body of the church in the Western world. The numerical results of our decline are already devastating, but perhaps the downturn is not limited only to our numbers.

Ruth and I were in a North African refugee camp. For 160,000 of the people of Western Sahara, this place had been their home for more than thirty years. Their meagre diet (averaging around 300 calories a day) was mainly provided by a variety of concerned agencies, including some churches. You can imagine our shame when we were shown a storehouse containing some church contributions. There were bags and bags of unwanted raisins, accompanied by a large volume of soup mix which had been rejected by US consumers, and because unsaleable and devoid of commercial value was therefore deemed to be an appropriate expression of Christian generosity and compassion for refugees exiled to the Sahara desert.

Perhaps some folks might be forgiven for concluding that, not only is the numerical quantity of Western Christianity declining in the twenty-first century, but also its quality as well.

So, Will the Church Die?

Graham Kendrick and I were making our way around some fifty UK cities (in only sixty-four days!) on the 1978 'Fighter' tour. I can remember pointing to the sobering statistics of unremitting decline in church attendance over a seventy-year period. Highlighting the present trend, I predicted the British evangelical churches would have become extinct by the dawn of the twenty-first century.

That disaster, of course, never happened. A renaissance of Christian commitment intervened – but such renewal needs to happen in every generation if the church is to regain its effectiveness in Western society.

Never has this been more important than right now.

The church in other parts of the world has also had to face up to the possibility of premature extermination, but for very different reasons. Time and again, the Lord Jesus has intervened to save his church. Nowhere, in recent times, has his involvement been more evident than in the virulent HIV/Aids epidemic sweeping across Africa.

As people have faced up to that awful testing certificate with the word 'positive' upon it, they have turned their lives over to the only one who has ever conquered death. Instead of wasting the closing years of their lives, many people have employed them to tell their fellow HIV/Aids sufferers how they too can find Jesus.

Let's look at a single situation, which is just one among thousands. Jennifer, a Kenyan woman, was weeping, and she was dying. There were two or three years of life left for her at the very most.

Jennifer was brought up to go to church. She believed in Jesus, but that belief touched her head and understanding more than it did her lifestyle. As time passed, she found a husband and settled into married life, but soon her problems began.

After eight years of married life, there were still no children, which is a disastrous situation in much of African culture. Eventually, the marriage broke down and ended in divorce.

Jennifer's next chapter of life revolved around a saga of prostitution to support herself. She lived in Ongata Rongai, a slum on the outskirts of Nairobi, Kenya. Living there, her prostitution would not give her great economic advantages, because a girl sells her body there for about twenty-five to thirty cents a time. Throughout this phase of her life, she continued to go to church and believe in God — but it was a lightly-held belief, not a life-changing one.

From her brief liaisons, she became pregnant on three separate occasions. She is unable to tell any of the children the identity of their father.

Eventually, Jennifer became very sick. After an acute bout of illness in March of 2004, she was tested and identified as being HIV positive. At this moment, she finally woke up to the truth of how she had been living. Faced with the reality, and the imminence, of her eternal destiny, she finally surrendered her life to Jesus Christ.

Now she weeps, not because she has found Jesus, but for the wasted years. She had known the truth for so long, but only in her head. She had never allowed it to penetrate her heart and her life. Now she has done so, and she uses every available moment to tell others of this Jesus she has found, and how they can discover his love for themselves. Her tubercular cough wracks her frail body, and the tears flow freely as she pleads with others to give their lives to Jesus when they are healthy, not sick, so that the best days of their lives may be lived for him. She longs for others to learn from her mistakes. In her case, she is very sorry that all she can give to the Lord are the shattered fragments of a broken life.

Soon she will be home. But we must ask if we have learned how to die from an African church that we once first taught where to find eternal life? Have we learned that the church is much larger than ourselves? Do we understand that the church can never die? As the Salvation Army has always pointed out, we do not die, we can only be 'promoted to Glory'!

Notes

1. C. Calver, *Descending Like a Dove* (Orlando, Charisma, 2003)
2. C. Calver, *Alive In the Spirit* (Orlando, Charisma, 2005)

CHAPTER EIGHT

Untame the Wildness (Gavin)

It was a lovely midsummer evening: the air was light, the sun was still up and its beams were pouring down in an incredible display of splendour. But I was located in the middle of the English countryside leading a Youth for Christ residential at an outdoor activity centre. The location was beautiful but the work was hard. However, I have always loved residential courses and find it incredible how you can do the equivalent of a year's worth of local church youth work in a few days or a week. On this particular occasion we were engaged in a great game of football. There were about fifty young people aged around eleven and twelve, and ten leaders. The match followed a regular favoured format of the leaders against the young people.

I used to be quite good at football (soccer) but I have since been seriously injured, and am also not quite so fit and lean as I used to be. I still play in an evangelistic football league, but today I am fundamentally trying to avoid kicking people too often in the name of Jesus! However, against young people I can become closer to Pelé than the old bruiser Vinnie Jones. The skills that would never work against a man can bamboozle a twelve-year-old. It's so wonderful for my self-esteem, and so terrible for theirs!

The game was going well and the so-called 'leaders' were winning. I was having the game of my life and just kept scoring goals. Eventually the young people were starting to get agitated and quite visibly frustrated – they knew that they had had enough. A young lad called Mickey began striding purposefully towards me. He was clearly the leader of the group. You may wonder how on earth I knew that this particular young man was the ringleader of his peers? Well, he was big for his age and used this to control his 'friends'. In short, he had muscles where a twelve-year-old should just have arms, a scar cut right across his forehead as a souvenir from one of his regular violent altercations, and as you looked into young Mickey's eyes he'd seen more hurt, difficulty and pain in his short life than I would see in my entire middle-class existence.

Mickey came right up to me, invading my personal space while attempting to be as threatening and imposing as possible. In an interestingly eclectic collection of language he informed me that it would be in my greater personal interests in regard to safety and presumably longevity to kindly refrain from scoring another goal! This was a somewhat shocking interchange to anyone listening in. But for myself, being in the regular business of evangelistic youth ministry, I was not going to be put off or intimidated. After all, Mickey was simply using a methodology with me that had helped him to look after himself successfully on previous occasions. The game continued.

Eventually I just happened to receive the ball around the centre circle. I dribbled round three pint-sized twelve-year-olds and then exchanged passes with another leader. On receiving the ball back I placed it into the bottom corner of the net. Goal! I didn't hit it too hard as we were playing with young people, although frankly I did feel for the scrawny eleven-year-old goalkeeper who tried in vain to dive across the goal and keep it out. I simply couldn't imagine what was to happen next.

Deeply angered by the fact that I had disobeyed his previous command, and disturbed further by being beaten by yet another goal, Mickey strode towards me exploding with real hate. As he moved closer I could see from both his body language and his venomous eyes that the sparks were beginning to rage inside him. He came up really close and drew a penknife from his sock. He held his playground weapon up to me saying that if I dared to score again then I would never walk again. There was no doubting from his words, poise and actions that, as far as he was concerned, his threat was real. He truly would guarantee this to be the case.

What on earth should I do now? I thought to myself. Every good youth ministry course and book would say that he should be sent home. I've taught myself on the need to discipline appropriately when situations have got out of hand. This particular scenario seemed untenable. In this instance a young person had acted threateningly towards an adult twice, and on the second occasion used a weapon. Surely for the good of the other young people as well as the residential as a whole I had to send him home? After all, how could anything positive come out of having him stay there with us for the rest of the time?

In truth, ninety-nine times out of 100 I would have sent him packing. However, today felt different, and I just could not explain why. As I looked at Mickey once more, and saw those eyes filled with a concoction of hate, anger and pain, I wondered what on earth I'd be sending him home to. What would be waiting for him when he returned prematurely due to misbehaviour and a total lack of self-discipline? Something in my spirit felt that no good could possibly be achieved by sending him home. How could he ever be helped if he continued to be turned away by those who could offer him his one chance? After all, most of his behaviour was as a direct result of the nurture he had incurred. No young person is all bad but they do bear the scars of adult damage inflicted on an already 'fallen' human nature.

I quickly dealt with the immediate situation by removing the knife from Mickey's hand. He thought he was physically imposing, and for his age he was: but there are times when it does help to be six foot three inches and sixteen stone! I then explained to Mickey that we were going to let him stay. He was clearly expecting to be sent home, and it was an incredible moment to see the look on his face as I informed him otherwise.

For a young man so used to consistent rejection he simply couldn't comprehend quite why we were allowing him to remain at the residential. This smallest token of grace shown to this troubled young person blew him away. He had never known what it was to not be scorned, spat upon and rejected for messing up.

In spite of his surprise and unbridled joy at being allowed to stay, Mickey's normal behaviour resumed pretty quickly. For the rest of the residential he was simply the biggest pain that I have ever encountered in youth ministry. He was fighting, swearing, encouraging others to break all the rules, and in need of constant supervision. It was as if every action he undertook had been scripted towards disrupting the residential for every other young person in attendance. Mickey needed far more oversight than anyone else. During one meeting we had the unlikely ratio of forty-five young people being supervised by two leaders whilst Mickey had four leaders all to himself.

It came to the last night of the course and I was preaching the evangelistic message. Being an evangelist can be difficult. In one sense you are fundamentally in the rejection ministry. For every person who says you're right and chooses to follow Jesus, ten may do the opposite. This means that you can't help but feel extremely vulnerable and on edge. Calling people to follow Jesus and make a physical response to the call will never cease to frighten me, no matter how many times I do it.

In addition it was the height of summer and I am someone who sweats a fair deal. Sometimes after preaching in a marquee in the middle of August I feel like I've been swimming and lost a stone! This all meant that by the time I'd preached the gospel and offered people the chance to respond I found myself feeling very hot and vulnerable whilst standing in my own personal pool of Siloam.

As soon as I finished my talk and gave an opportunity for young people to respond I headed quickly for the exit, desperate to feel the coolness of the outside air. As the door drew closer and closer I saw Mickey stand up and make a bee-line for me. Everything within me was longing for him to go away and leave me alone. After all surely he just wanted to cause trouble – again. I secretly hoped that I might get outside before Mickey could get anywhere near me. I increased my pace but his purposeful stride helped him reach me first. I felt myself saying inside 'Go away. I don't like you and I'm pretty sure that Jesus doesn't either!' I really couldn't face the hassle of Mickey at that moment.

Before I could duck his gaze he opened his mouth and said, 'Gavin, can I pray with you? I've just given my life to Jesus.' My jaw dropped so rapidly it felt like it might hit the floor. What an incredible moment! I simply wasn't expecting Mickey to say that. It's times like these that, whether you call yourself an evangelist or not you realise that none of this has anything to do with you. It's all down to the sovereignty of God. I simply stood there in sheer disbelief at the wonder of this Jesus who yet again was in the business of changing lives. I prayed for Mickey and helped him to confess his sins and surrender his life to Jesus. This was such a great privilege; nothing in life is anywhere near as energising, enthralling and exhilarating as praying for someone as they surrender their life to the Lord Jesus for the first time.

We finished praying and I was about to turn and pray with some other young people when to my utter surprise Mickey started to pray. Having not been socialised into church he had no understanding of the mechanics of this so he paced around with his eyes wide open and bellowed quickly: 'Dear Jesus, thank you for Gavin. He's good at football. Amen.' It was a surreal prayer but one of the most significant ones that anyone has ever prayed over me. Here was a lad with no hope, direction or meaning and yet he'd met Jesus. Life wasn't suddenly perfect but he had the Way, the Truth and the Life to help him.

The best thing is that the story doesn't end there. Mickey was from a church youth group on a council estate in the north of England. Prior to the course, neither he nor any of the other thirty-nine regular attendees had made any kind of commitment to follow Jesus Christ. Six weeks after these events I received an email from Mickey's youth worker, sharing of hers and Mickey's frustration that they were still waiting for the last two in the youth group to come to Jesus! Thirty-seven of Mickey's friends had become Christians as a direct result of him going home and sharing what had happened to him.

Something about the change in this young leader led to great change in the lives of so many others. So often that's the case. Remove one blockage and a stream can flow – it is the way that God's Spirit will often move – and orchestrate incredible results.

Irrelevant?

The wonderful thing about Mickey was that he remained relevant to those other young people on his estate. The transformation in him helped point others to Jesus. He didn't return to his home and find that he had nothing in common with his peers. If anything the situation was quite the reverse. Mickey had met Jesus and with dogged determination he made sure that everyone else was given the same incredible opportunity to meet him too. Just like John the Baptist in John 1, Mickey was able to act as a signpost pointing others to Jesus.

Somehow we must fight to stay relevant to people in all manner of backgrounds and situations so that we can finally see the world changed and won for Christ. The terrifying thing is that, in contrast to Mickey, so often someone becomes a Christian and is immediately irrelevant to all of those who they lived around before. It is rightly observed that often the first thing you lose as a Christian is your non-Christian friends. All of a sudden all the friends are from church. So for a new believer most of their social time is spent at church events and their music and literature is all that of the church. Now some of this is good, and obviously lifestyle change must come about as a result of becoming a Christian. However, it seems to take someone about six months to lose touch with the world from which they came. This can't be right!

Is it not possible for our lives to change and yet we can still return to our old environment to be salt and light within it? There are clear dangers here, and church will need to be different in order to help this happen. But for the sake of the kingdom a new approach to fresh converts is vital.

It is true that when we encounter Jesus our lives become unrecognisable, yet at the same time it is fundamental to remain active amongst those who don't yet know the good news. The story of Zacchaeus in Luke 19 is a wonderful illustration. Here was a man who had cheated those in need and shamelessly taken advantage of his position as chief tax collector in order for personal gain. He wanted to observe who Jesus was, but being diminutive in stature he couldn't see over the crowd. Therefore, he climbed a sycamore tree in order to get a glimpse of the King. Jesus called him down and declared 'I must stay at your house today' (verse 5). This caused great shock, as the crowd couldn't believe that Jesus had chosen to be the guest of such a sinner.

Zacchaeus had been a terrible man but when he met Jesus everything changed. He surrendered his life to the King, and put his hand in his pocket. This was an incredibly significant action as he had spent his life thus far cheating people of their money, not giving it out. He pledged to repay the many who he had cheated and instead of simply meeting the restitutional requirement of 20 per cent Zacchaeus paid back 400 per cent! I'm sure that after this incredible encounter he did not go and hide in the church. Zacchaeus would have remained amongst the people who must have been stunned by this incredible change. He would have been 'in' the world, but not compromised by it. He would have had to remain in the world in order to repay the many victims of his greed. Mickey was much the same. He was turned inside out, upside down and back to front by his encounter with Jesus yet also remained amongst his peers, who hadn't yet met the King.

What I love about Mickey is he didn't wait for the church to come up with a four-pronged strategy for outreach, he didn't wait for permission to share, and he didn't sit in anticipation of an imminent word of prophecy that he was to be an evangelist. He just got up and told his tribe about Jesus.

Mickey's story is somewhat reminiscent of when the Samaritan woman met Jesus in John 4. Here is a woman of little moral fibre, a woman whom no one really likes, and a woman who goes to collect water in the inconvenience of the heat of the day, hoping to avoid the scorn and derision of others. But she does meet someone at the well: Jesus. After requesting a drink that he never gets, Jesus eventually gives her living water. She becomes the first Gentile Christian and then goes running back to her village to tell everyone what has happened. As a result the entire village then comes running across the fields to meet Jesus.

There must have been such an incredible change in this woman. Even though the odds were stacked against her and her testimony would be unlikely to be accepted, something so miraculous had transformed her that the inhabitants of the town forgot the footpath and ran across the fields just to get to Jesus. Nothing was allowed to impede their progress, and stop them from getting to him. Just like the Samaritan woman, Mickey was the unlikeliest of people. Again, the change in him when he met Jesus was so significant that those who had known him previously were impacted and wanted to know this Jesus.

A Watered-down Version?

As a church we've got to allow people to remain relevant to those in the world and share with them. We have to release people. It is not good enough to have young people like Mickey becoming Christians and then to instruct them to have nothing in common with those who do not yet know Jesus. Too often the church can seem to sanitise our passion and get rid of so much of what might be infectious to the world. I hear endless accounts of young men in particular who struggle deeply with the church. According to such men the church appears to emasculate them. There seems to be something so effeminate in both the style of how things are done and the understanding of God. Yes, he is a God of love and compassion, but he's also a God of power and justice. Jesus wept at Lazarus's tomb but then raised him to life (John 11). Jesus felt great sorrow over Jerusalem (Luke 13:31–35) but also turned over the temple courts (Matthew 21:12–16). Why do we so often only focus on the soft side? The pain should result in passion and change – not merely learning to live with the pain!

It is no wonder that we have fewer men in the church than ever before. In the 18–30 age bracket it is frequently alleged that women outnumber the men by as much as seven to one! In addition the men that we do have in the church are a generation who are often unsure of their identity within the Bride of Christ. No wonder I hear so many women within the church complaining that they perceive all Christian men as being either married or wet fish! We need to encourage the church to take risks and see the Christian life as an adventure. This gets us away from a sanitised and watered down version of what it means to be Christians. It takes us back to what it was like for the early church.

The Christian life is not a systematic set of problems and rules but something so much more exciting than that. John Eldridge puts it this way in his book, *Wild at Heart*:

Life is not a problem to be solved; it is an adventure to be lived. That's the nature of it and has been since the beginning when God set the dangerous stage for this high-stakes drama and called the whole wild enterprise good. He rigged the world in such a way that it only works when we embrace risk as the theme of our lives, which is to say, only when we live by faith.[1]

Somewhere along the journey of the Western church, everything appears to have become a bit too safe. I dream of Christians being liberated to fully live this adventure, to know the high-stakes nature of life, and to live with greater faith. A wild generation who make the most of their opportunities, live on the edge and show what it is to put faith in Jesus above everything else in the world. A renewed breed of Christians who are so dramatically changed by an encounter with the living Jesus that those around can't help but be transformed as well.

I long for a generation of Christians who, like Mickey, find Jesus and are then compelled to share their findings with those who don't yet know the King. A people who have the faith to witness to their peers and see them saved. A generation who don't just see church attendance as important but believe with everything in them that mission must take place in the world. Individuals who know what it is to be a part of church yet don't become tamed by it. Brave men and women who see life as the adventure that it is and don't become lost from the high-stakes drama by being socialised into church. Put simply, I long for a generation of transformed Mickeys.

Notes

1. J. Eldridge, *Wild at Heart* (Nashville, Thomas Nelson Inc., 2001) p. 200

CHAPTER NINE

Learning to Love
(Clive)

Picture the bridegroom on his wedding
day. The music plays softly while he waits
for his bride to appear. Then the best man nudges him and
he glances lovingly over his shoulder in anticipation of seeing his beautiful bride — only to be greeted by an arm
bounding up the aisle, closely followed by two or three
toes, and perhaps a fingernail. Closing in quickly from
behind, there is an elbow joint or two, the torso, and then
a head rolling up alone. Even though the scene appears
ridiculous and disgusting, the so-called 'body of Christ' can
look similar, at least to the casual observer.

Scripture goes even further, for the church is regularly
referred to as the 'bride of Christ'. Continuing this analogy,
Paul is quite explicit in his claim that the Corinthian church
is betrothed to Jesus Christ. This flawed, weak, divided and
desperately needy body of believers is actually engaged to be
married to the King of kings. She is pledged in love to him
(2 Corinthians 11:2). This theme is continued in Paul's letter
to the Christians in Ephesus where he explains that the highest attitude of a husband to his wife is a reflection of the love
that Jesus Christ possesses for his church (Ephesians 5:25).

In due time, Jesus is going to take the church to be his
bride. He intends that we live and reign with him forever.
We are those for whom he died, and therefore have
received his love and forgiveness. Frequently, however, we
have fallen into the trap of limiting the bride of Christ. We
think that the church consists of just our local

congregation, but we can actually anticipate spending eternity with vast multitudes of people who may be very different from ourselves. Because we share the same heavenly Father, each person is also one of our brothers and sisters.

To a world which continually demanded to see a miracle, or at the very least, a sign, Jesus left the greatest wonder of all. He performed not simply a physical healing, or a feeding of 5,000 men (and probably an equal number of women and children); he did not just subject a storm to his will, or even just arise from the dead. Instead, he asked his Father four times that his people might be one in their love and commitment (see John 17). His desire was that old and young, rich and poor, upper class and lower class, all might transcend these differences and truly be one church.

The heart desire of Jesus was that the church of Christ be the one place in society where there was no racial discrimination, class preference, or generation gap; where there was no sexism, ageism, racism, or any kind of division at all.

This unity was to be the greatest miracle of all. He yearned for a society of all kinds of different people, yet bonded together in loving commitment as one body, because they loved and served the same Lord Jesus Christ. He ordained that the way this world would really know who he is, would not be by the propagation of right doctrine, nor by the performance of correct ritual, but by the way in which we as Christians love one another. Today our unity is to be the classic demonstration of the truth of the way that the Lord Jesus is at work creating a different kind of society, in which people live in his world in the way he desired.

Living in unity as Christ intended is the only way we can reveal the glorious status of the church as the body of Jesus here on earth, and as his future bride in heaven. If we fail to love our fellow Christians, how can we claim to show God's glory to the world?

An Alternative Community

Imagine living at a time when genuine hostilities broke out in the Western world against the church of Jesus Christ. Envision a great persecution where our brothers and sisters were daily being seized, taken away, and herded into over-crowded prisons. Suppose our local fellowship were on trial and accused of being a dangerously committed body of Christian believers – fully in love with the Lord Jesus and with each other.

In reality, many people today are looking for the evidence of that new, alternative society. Just 150 years after the death of Jesus, the church historian Tertullian recorded that the pagans accused Christians of just about everything that their imaginations could devise: incest, because they 'loved their brothers and sisters', atheism, because they rejected as bogus all gods other than their own, cannibalism for 'eating the Lord's body', and drunken orgies because of their 'love feasts' and 'fellowship meals' together.

Yet Tertullian says that there was one thing which the local pagans were not able to ignore, for they kept exclaiming in amazement, 'See how these Christians love one another!'

A well-known phrase is 'Seeing is believing'. In Tertullian's day, the quality of Christian relationships made a huge impact. Two thousand years have passed, and we need to ask if those types of relationships still exist today.

To answer this question, let's get down to a practical level. How could a Christian lifestyle totally amaze a non-Christian in current times? What would make an impact in today's society?

As Madonna reminds us, 'We live in a material world'.

Suppose that you discover that your brother or sister in Christ has insufficient money, food or possessions, and you have more than you really need. Try sharing what you have.

Let's be even more specific. What about the money building up in your bank account when your sister is a single parent, struggling for survival? What about the car in your garage when your brother needs transport because his vehicle has been written off in a road accident? What about the individual who is lonely because no one ever invites him to visit for a meal? What about the spare bed when someone needs somewhere to stay? Whether or not we are threatened or challenged by such suggestions – the evidence begins to accumulate by the answers to these questions.

Yes, of course, there are non-Christians who can claim to live generous lives – and without Jesus. Yet there is something gloriously anarchic about the Holy Spirit, when he provokes a degree of generosity that represents true Christian living that can rarely be matched elsewhere.

Ultimately, the degree to which we demonstrate the reality of God's love working among us will come down to our own attitude, and to the sense of gratitude that we have for all God has given to us as individuals. Only then can we begin to demonstrate a different set of values that truly forge a genuine demonstration of community between us. President John F. Kennedy once stated that, 'If a free society cannot help the many who are poor, it cannot save the few who are rich.' As the church, we need to take note!

There are glorious moments when the church truly lives up to her calling. Take this story of two young people who met each other at university in York, which is a Roman-walled city in the north of England. Kevin was studying German, and Sue was taking her degree in mathematics. Both were Christians and mutually attracted to each other.

To cut a long story short, they fell in love, and then married. After university and the wedding, they settled down to a life of wedded bliss, working as teachers in a Midlands town.

Things were going well for them financially, and they had a lovely house (plus mortgage), with great furniture, and a whole range of wedding presents. They had also started a youth work with many of the kids from their school. A mission at the local church linked up with their work, and a young evangelist, who was part of the mission team, stayed for two weeks in their home with them.

A few weeks later, they asked the evangelist to come back to visit them. This young couple then told him they were planning to give up their teaching positions and head off for Bible college to be properly trained and equipped to fulfil the calling that they felt the Lord was laying on their lives. They were going to Niger, West Africa, with Wycliffe Bible Translators, where Kevin would use his linguistic gifts to translate the New Testament into the Kenori language.

Their major problem was to figure out what they should do with the house, the furniture, and the wedding presents. Both sets of parents refused to accept the property, and they were strongly urged by well-meaning friends to sell their house, holding the money for a rainy day. However, they felt that the Lord was calling them to give all that they possessed to the young evangelist and his wife, who had no home of their own.

When he was given the news, the young evangelist could scarcely believe it, and nor could the members of the local church that this couple attended. Such generosity and obedience seemed to be quite unparalleled, and many people found this action to be a real challenge to their own level of commitment to Jesus. Kevin and Sue were less bothered! They felt that everything they owned was a gift from God, and entrusted into their care as his stewards. Therefore, the real issue did not lie in what they should give, but in how much they should keep.

Later, just before they were to begin their two-year training at Bible college, they faced a major problem. The college had no available accommodation remaining for married students, so Kevin and Sue had nowhere to live. Then God intervened. He provided a little country cottage near the college, with its own tennis court and swimming pool – and all for £6.00 (about $12) a week!

After Bible college, they went to Niger, translated the New Testament, and then returned to Britain to train others at the Wycliffe Centre. However, they brought back more than they had taken. Although they were medically diagnosed as being unable to have children, the Lord had suspended the laws of nature on a couple of occasions, and two very healthy young lads were the result. This 'miracle' proves that when you give something to God, he returns the favour!

When they returned home for their new teaching role, the Lord once again provided for them, but this time they were on the receiving end of the gift of a house and furniture. Eventually, they moved back to serve in West Africa. In case you think that this is just another missionary story, embellished over the years, and much too good to be true, I need to say that I was the young evangelist. My wife, Ruth, and I were the recipients of the house, the furniture, and wedding presents, so we know the story is true!

The lesson this couple learned was a very important one: they knew that ultimately they were each part of a small nuclear family, as well as part of a worldwide family, and they had responsibilities to both. The world deserves to see the reality of Christian love in action, and in this case, they did! The impact on the school where they worked, and the local church that they attended, can only be imagined. When we as Christians are prepared to relinquish our possessions and live life under the direct control of the King of kings, our commitment to Christ, and our relationships, will speak volumes.

We are called to live in a dynamic partnership together, sharing our material needs, our problems, our anxieties, our fears and our blessings. As the Lord Jesus instructed, 'Little children, let us not love merely in theory or in speech but in deed and in truth (in practice and sincerity)' (1 John 3:18, Amplified Bible).

If we live out this verse, let's face it – conviction will be the certain result!

You'll Never Walk Alone

For much too long we have informed young converts that when they become Christians, Jesus comes to live in their lives, but we have told them little more. We may add that he brings forgiveness for their sin and introduces his new lifestyle. We have forgotten to add that they also become part of a company of believers. God's plan is brothers and sisters joined together in his family. We might find each other to be a little difficult, and we might not have chosen one another, but we are lumbered with each other! Suddenly we have acquired millions of brothers and sisters, not just for now, but also for eternity.

We might well ask if Christianity, therefore, destroys our individuality.

No way, for the Lord Jesus establishes a personal relationship with each one of us when he takes up residence within our individual lives, not leaving us to cope alone. The greatest gift that he gives us, apart from his Holy Spirit, is the love, support and encouragement of each other.

The intention of the living God is that the majority of us would never be satisfied existing as isolated individuals. The solitary lifestyle is a privilege reserved only for a handful of extraordinary people. Most of us can discover what it means to be fully human only when we are living alongside others as part of a community.

Amazingly, this basis for relationships is found in the nature and character of God himself, since he declared, 'Let us make man in our image' (Genesis 1:26). This announcement reveals a God who is in permanent relationship with himself. God is a community of three equal persons, who relate to each other in love (John 17:24), vividly demonstrating perfect unity. God cannot be divided from himself, and he intended the same for us!

We must never forget that our God is a personal God. Just as he relates to us, so we are to build relationships with one another. Simply put, from God's point of view, he designed us to be part of a community.

As John Wesley rode along on his horse one day, the story goes, a man galloped up alongside him. As they fell into conversation, the man taught Wesley a lesson that he would never forget. The words that made such an impact on John Wesley were, 'Sir, you wish to serve God and go to heaven. You must find companions or make them, for the Bible knows nothing about solitary religion.'

We often concentrate our energies on being individuals, when our Lord looks for a community. However, he does not intend to reduce our individual personality, rather he wants to fulfil us. He knows that what we can never find alone, we can experience together. Loving one another is foundational, because without that loving commitment, we will function at a fraction of our full potential.

Often we attempt to live out our Christian lives in a solitary manner, like a big toe running up the road, divorced from the rest of the body. Frankly, we need each other. As Paul wrote, 'If the whole body were an eye, where would the sense of hearing be?' (1 Corinthians 12:17). In the very same way, each of us has different functions to carry out in the body of Christ. None of us is meant to be God's answer to everything and everybody, but instead, we are to live and work together.

The independence we so overtly practice grieves the heart of God. If we undertake a project, a mission, or an event, we so often fail to ask who else might be doing something similar, and then work together. We do not ask because we do not want to know! We would rather run something ourselves and have our own little independent work, rather than join in with someone else, despite that together we achieve much more.

This scenario is where the words 'my ministry' intrude. I hate that phrase! After all, if it is ministry, then it isn't mine – and if it is mine, then how can it really be ministry? This kind of individualism is not consistent with the teaching of scripture, where the word 'saints' occurs sixty-one times, but 'saint' (singular) is found only once.

Similarly, there are twenty-one letters in the New Testament, but only three are addressed to individuals. All the rest were written to churches, so naturally the concerns they express concentrate on the quality of relationships that existed between their readers. Unlike the content of many sermons today, the biblical writers appear to be more concerned with corporate relationships than individual behaviour.

In God's Word, Christians are constantly urged to demonstrate their sense of mutual responsibility and commitment to 'one another'. We are instructed to 'love each other deeply' (1 Peter 4:8), 'serve one another in love'

(Galatians 5:13), and 'spur one another on towards love and good deeds' (Hebrews 10:24).

We are also admonished to 'pray for each other' (James 5:16), 'forgive whatever grievances you may have against one another' (Colossians 3:13), and 'Honour one another' (Romans 12:10).

Additionally, we are to 'look...to the interests of others' (Philippians 2:4), 'Cheerfully share your home' (1 Peter 4:9, NLT), and above all, 'encourage one another daily' (Hebrews 3:13).

This pattern of behaviour does not have a finishing line, as this sense of family does not just last for now, but forever. Therefore, even our burial cannot intervene to destroy this oneness, because the church of Jesus Christ is the only society on earth that has never lost a single one of its members through death!

Living Up to Our Message

If Christianity were a religion to which a mental assent alone was required, then there would be room within it for those with cold, unfeeling hearts. However, the Christian faith can never be reduced to an unfeeling, academic theology. Christianity is not about a doctrine, but essentially about a person.

The question can never be 'What do we know about him?' (that is, in our head), but must be 'What does he mean to us?' (that is, in our heart). Christianity is not a religion about God, but a relationship with him, and the reality of this claim is witnessed by the depth of our love for each other. In the USA, this concept would be summarized as 'learning to walk your talk'.

Our faith must always transcend the level of words alone. The people of God must, in their relationships, reveal the glory of the living God to the world in which they live. That glory is not just revealed through an individual, but through the corporate identity of a people who belong to Jesus.

We need to recognise that we are never going to convince people by intellectual argument alone. For so long, the people have been *told* the gospel. We have threatened, cajoled, argued and preached; then we have offered special services, concerts, baptisms and films. Hundreds of thousands of words have been uttered; hundreds of thousands of pounds or dollars spent; yet our lands remain stubbornly pagan.

We need to admit that words have never been enough. If the kingdom is truly here, and the living God is at work among us, then the time has come to show people the reality, instead of just talk. As Jesus said, 'By this all men will know that you are my disciples, if you love one another' (John 13:35).

Imagine the reaction if people around us truly saw Christian love and fellowship being exhibited in practical ways. How would they respond if they witnessed us caring for the older members of the congregation by doing the shopping for them when they were unable to get out of the house, or by spending an hour sitting and talking to keep them company, or by working in the garden when they were too frail to keep it as nice as it had once been?

Here in Connecticut, I am thrilled to be part of a church where so many offer their practical skills in help and support of one another. In fact, on one day of each year, some six hundred of the members join with other local churches and 'blitz' the local community. Many folks unable to pay for such services are amazed to have their houses decorated, renovated or repaired. Gardens are remodelled and refuse collected. Nourishing food is prepared for everyone. Best of all, links are established with those who would never dream that 'church' could have any direct relevance to their lives.

The truth stands that in many of our churches, we have practical gifts and talents which we could be giving to one another. This impactful, all-day event has made people in our own church more aware of what putting Christian love into action really means.

If only we could get involved in actively loving and caring *for* one another. If only we could stop living as 'islands', and instead, function as a body. What a difference we would make! Perhaps one day the accountant will, as a normal event, do the mechanic's accounts *for* him, while the mechanic mends the accountant's car. The contact brings fellowship, both jobs are done *free* of charge, and the world loses 30 per cent!

Our activities can never be artificially divided into two tidily organised compartments labelled 'secular' or 'spiritual', because everything we have was designed to be offered in worship. Our surrender to Jesus Christ has made our whole lives a contribution to others, because, as Jesus pointed out, whatever we do for them simply becomes an act of service to the King of kings.

Walking in the Light – Together

In the light of such active service, we are not surprised Jesus agreed with the statement that to love God and our neighbour was the greatest commandment (Luke 10:27–28).

If we are called to love our neighbour as ourselves when they are not Christians, how much more beauty should be seen in the relationships between Christian brothers and sisters? Such relationships should be so beautiful that those observing from outside will be staggered and amazed.

But, let's be honest, how often do people gaze in wonder at our love for one another?

Or, how often do we really put the feelings and needs of others above our own?

And just how concerned are we for each other, let alone for those people that we just do not seem to like?

All in all, just how much genuine love, commitment and encouragement do we really give each other?

These are tough questions; and let's face it, Sunday by Sunday, thousands leave our churches as the pastor shakes hands at the door and asks 'How are you?' Inevitably back comes the all-embracing reply, 'Fine'. Despite the way which we truly feel, we always try to keep the intelligent enquirer at arm's length. Sometimes we would rather keep our problems to ourselves; more often we are scared to share ourselves. One could reconstruct that Sunday morning conversation adding the speaker's real thoughts in brackets.

'How are you?'

'I'm fine' (I feel lousy really).

'How's the wife?'

'She's fine' (Why on earth I married that woman I just cannot imagine).

'How are the children?'

'They're fine' (They are also the reason the wife's in such a state, 'Scream, scream, scream', especially the little one).

'And how's your job?'

'Fine' (You stupid...don't you know half the firm was laid off last week?).

'And how's your spiritual life?'

'Fine' (With that lot going on what on earth do you think it's like?).

Such dishonesty is not confined to the congregation. One Sunday night a few years ago, a young married couple was asked at the door of a Baptist church, by a pastor I knew, how they were doing.

When they confessed that things were really dreadful, and that they did not know how to cope, he swiftly brushed them off with a 'Fine, good evening,' because he could not handle the problems either.

Behind the plastic grin, many of us can be dishonest by smiling to cover up the deep hurt which we feel inside. If only we were able to open up ourselves to one another and realise that God never intended us to struggle alone.

Not only should we resist being 'loners', but we should also allow ourselves to actually become vulnerable to one another. If the Christian community was equipped to minister to our genuine hurts and problems, how different things could be.

In sharing ourselves, we begin to expose the real person inside us. Then we can expel the residue of inner bitterness and resentment and start to live joyfully as the community of faith. This openness brings new friendships and a new depth of communication. Is this not the way the body of Christ was always supposed to be? We know that 'if we walk in the light, as he is in the light, we have fellowship with one another, and the blood of Jesus...cleanses us from all sin' (1 John 1:7).

When we remove the sham, we are free to be ourselves, and we escape the pressure of immediately being transformed into total Christ-likeness. Then together as people of God, we can journey on towards our goal in God.

Forgiveness Rules – OK?

We can let forgiveness rule, only if we are prepared to forgive the past. Many of us have learned to tolerate long-standing problems with our fellow Christians, a fundamental mistake.

The story is told of the apostle John when he was living as an elderly man in Ephesus. Transportation was provided for him by means of a stretcher, carried by two of the younger (and stronger) Christians. As he passed through the marketplace, John would spot groups of Christians, and he would continually call out, 'Little children, love one another'.

Slightly embarrassed at these loud comments, those carrying him asked why he kept on repeating himself. They wondered if the sun or old age was affecting him. The apostle's reply was succinct: 'Because the Master commanded it and because this is the first foundation on which all else is built'.

This theme of love infected John's epistles. He asked how we can claim to love God if we do not love our brothers and sisters' (1 John 3:10, 4:20–21). This love is not limited to our words, but must be demonstrated by our actions (1 John 3:18). The one potential impediment could be our lack of forgiveness.

Taking the attitude that we just don't get on with someone, and using that as a justification for having problems with them, is not acceptable. Of course, God made us all so different in our character that we won't automatically get on with everybody. However, Jesus commands us to love one another, and he does not tell us to do something without giving us the strength to carry it out.

Some relationships will be harder to form than others: some will just fall into place, and others will take months of working out. Often the relationships between those of opposite characters which require work prove to be the deepest and most profitable. We cannot excuse ourselves by saying we just don't get on. If we both want to, and we open ourselves to God's direction, then we will. 'If you have problems with people – you have problems!' is well quoted.

People problems particularly crop up when someone hurts us. Often we see that particular instance as a deliberate attack upon us, and yet, if we shared our feelings with the person concerned, they would be horrified to find that we had taken it that way. Frequently, the cause could be no more than a misunderstanding, a throwaway comment, or a harmless joke. Now forgiveness needs to come in – after all, everyone can make a mistake.

However, even if someone deliberately hurts us, we have no right to overreact in what we might excuse as 'righteous indignation', and cut off any contact with them. Have we not often prayed as Jesus taught, 'Father...forgive us the wrong we have done, in exactly the same way that we have forgiven those who have wronged us?' Those prayers have been heard, and Jesus replies, 'If you forgive men when they sin against you, your heavenly Father will also forgive you. But if you do not forgive men their sins, your Father will not forgive your sins' (Matthew 6:14–15).

Perhaps time has come for us to go up to those in our congregation to whom we have never talked and open up communication. Maybe the moment has arrived to approach those against whom we harbour resentment, bitterness or past problems, to confess and get right with one another.

Are we now ready to demonstrate community in practical terms by learning to appreciate and support one another?

Are we ready to quietly commit ourselves to love, trust and serve one another?

After all is said and done, we must live as the church that is also called to be the bride of the King of kings.

CHAPTER TEN

Reaching and Supporting the Young (Gavin)

'**I want an exciting job** like yours, Gav,' Mark said. Now Mark was only fifteen, he had just heard me preach at a conference, and yet he had decided that he wanted my job. I tried to explain to Mark the realities of a travelling ministry: leaving your house in the ridiculously early hours, travelling hundreds of miles to talk for half an hour, and then coming home. The look on his face rapidly changed as the reality dawned on him that my world is not always that glamorous or exciting and he might not really be so keen on wanting a piece of it.

I wish that people like Mark could see how hard Christian leadership, national responsibilities and itinerant speaking can be. I guess that then both prayer support and understanding could be more tangible and realistic. It is a real privilege to do it, but no one should ever regard it as a 'walk in the park'.

It was on one such Sunday that I set off early in the morning and drove the best part of two hundred miles. On arrival at the church I was greeted very warmly and made to feel at home. As a travelling speaker you always notice new and different things at each destination. From the shops in a town, the style of housing and ethnic make up to the church building itself, the type of people in the church and the warmth of the reception. It is fascinating to visit many different places. The thing that struck me most on this particular occasion was that there seemed to be many young people wandering around the streets of the town and yet there were no teenagers whatsoever in the church and only a small smattering of younger children.

The church service itself passed quickly. The congregation seemed to have sympathised with my message of the desperate need to work with the next generation. Many responded positively to it and I had enjoyed the opportunity to be with them. After ending by sharing the Benediction I was very much looking forward to what I thought would be a well-deserved cup of coffee. Arriving in the dingy church hall at the back of the building I immediately noticed a tightly enclosed circle of four old ladies sat in the far right-hand corner. Although they were of a great vintage – probably all in their nineties – it was clear straight away that they ran the church. The vicar might believe that he was in charge but I was left in no doubt whatsoever that any church decisions would have to be approved by this self-appointed sub-committee.

Despite my anticipation of imminent coffee, and before I had even had time to grab a cup, one of these ladies of vintage shouted across to me firmly, 'Young man, over here, now!' I obeyed my order and a fifth chair was added to a now slightly wider, yet still enclosed, circle. The lady who had summoned me over began to rant with gusto, 'There are loads of young people in this community and yet none of them come to church. We pray for them every day but nothing is happening. We don't have anything in common with young people but we do want to see them here in church.' A second lady joined in, 'Young people are really different to us and there is nothing we can do about it even though we do want them to come to church.' A third lady added, 'We will continue to pray but we struggle as we can't imagine what else we can do.' The fourth and final lady finished without wasting a word, 'What are you going to do about it, Gavin?'

Somewhat taken aback by it all I spurted out, 'Not a great deal, as I live at least 189 miles away!' One of the ladies interjected, 'But something has to happen. We love these young people and yet we have nothing in common with them. If there was something we could do, we would.' Another added, 'Young people today are absolutely nothing like they used to be. We are helpless.'

It was at this point that I said something that was either incredibly brave or ridiculously stupid. I turned to the four ladies and simply asked: 'Have you never been through puberty?' As soon as I said it I wished that I hadn't and I could immediately see the colour leaving their faces. Attempting to rescue myself from what was fast becoming a rather desperate situation I spoke up. 'You see, the back-drop may be different but the fundamental changes that take place are the same. If you just think back to some of how you felt when you were young and reach out to this new generation in love then it will be amazing to think of what could happen.'

Within a matter of weeks these four old ladies had started a Rock Solid club (Rock Solid is a Youth for Christ outreach resource for use with unchurched 11- to 14-year-olds). They faithfully led it and desperately hoped to see some young people begin to engage with church. Within six months the group had over thirty young people going to it every week and the four key leaders were those wonderful vintage ladies! What a new generation of young people really needs are older people of all types, who are prepared to bother to try and help them. But to do this involves a crucial sacrifice. It entails being prepared to meet young people where they are, rather than where we want them to be. In other words, it means meeting them, instead of expecting everyone to come to us.

Old and Young Together

In research for my first book *Disappointed with Jesus?* I surveyed 200 young people about the type of youth leaders they would like. Over 85 per cent primarily wanted a parent/grandparent figure.[1] This destroys our strange theory that the best people to do youth ministry are the older brother/sister type. Often young people have siblings and older friends but what they are really lacking is a parent/grandparent type. It is into this sociological situation that a church full of parent and grandparent figures has an amazing missionary opportunity to a hurting generation of young people.

I love the potential within the church for the generations to serve one another. When you combine the enthusiasm of youth with the wisdom of age you have an amazing combination. The cost, as I've explained, is downward mobility on the part of those of us who are older. But then this would be an entirely mutually beneficial situation. I can think of many people who can become worn down and cynical through their experiences of church, yet when they see the vibrancy and enthusiasm of a young Christian it rubs off on them and the cynicism quickly falls away. Equally there are a myriad of younger Christians who benefit hugely from the help of those more mature in the faith. A church of all ages, shapes and sizes is a rich body that can make a radical difference – to themselves first, then to their community, their culture, and their world.

The church just has to take the needs of the young seriously. Most of us who come to faith do so as teenagers and it must be fundamental to any future growth and development of the church for us to reach out in love to a new generation. In a world where young people are more insecure than ever, we need the church to support and offer unqualified acceptance and love.

Equally, if the church still wants to be in healthy existence in the West in fifty years time then it must reach a new and younger audience. It is frightening to witness an ageing church. The same conferences are filled with the same people getting older every year. The church needs a new input of youth. Young people have the potential to take more risks. They have fewer commitments and are therefore able to try things that most of us wouldn't dare. The church desperately needs the vibrant cutting edge that a massive intravenous injection of younger people would produce. The results could be gloriously dangerous – but that is why our God has so often chosen those younger in Jesus to drive his people forward.

The Bible is littered with examples of old and young working together for the good of the kingdom. In Exodus 18, Moses needs some help. Even though he has faced the Lord at the burning bush (Exodus 3), and seen the Red Sea split before his eyes (Exodus 14), Moses needs some advice from someone who has been around a little longer. Into this situation steps his father-in-law, Jethro. He is upset to see that Moses is sitting alone as judge over all the people. Therefore he tells him to share the load. It is simply too much for Moses to hope to do on his own and Jethro's wisdom and experience make it easier for him to observe this in his son-in-law. Here is a man who has done amazing things, will soon receive the Ten Commandments from the top of Mount Sinai (Exodus 20) and yet even he needed a little gentle steering from an older head.

Further on in the Old Testament we come to the example of Elijah and Elisha. In 1 Kings 19, Elijah is at the end of his tether and he has retreated to a cave. The Lord appears to him with a simple question: 'what are you doing here, Elijah?' (1 Kings 19:9). In response Elijah says 'I have been very zealous for the Lord God Almighty. The Israelites have rejected your covenant, broken down your altars, and put your prophets to death with the sword. I am the only one left, and now they are trying to kill me too' (verse 10). Elijah can see no point in carrying on; he feels desolate and is ready to give up. So what does the Lord do? He gives him Elisha – a younger person to invest in. Elisha gives Elijah a new wave of enthusiasm, and Elijah gives Elisha the opportunity to become all he can be in God.

For all the many great instances within the Bible of multi-generational investment Jesus has to be the ultimate example of how it should be done. Jesus in his early thirties took on twelve younger men aged between fifteen and twenty-three. He lived amongst them, developed them, sought out their opinions, and gave them opportunities to do things even though he could do them better himself. He encouraged them to take risks (Matthew 14), used their efforts to great effect (John 6) and forgave the ultimate denial (John 21). When Jesus found and called his twelve disciples, what he really did was form the first youth group. Here was an older person bothering to invest in the up and coming when many others would have seen it as risky or too much like hard work. We may feel that we don't have enough time to invest in younger people, yet Jesus' three-year earthly ministry was primarily spent investing in younger people. Surely if Jesus made such a priority of passing on to others what he had to offer then we should find the time to do the same? Jesus gives us a wonderful example of what it means to develop a new generation.

Whatever angle you come at it from, young people need older people to invest in them. Whoever you are, whatever you're like, wherever you live, we must be giving support to those younger than ourselves. More than twenty-five years ago an adventurous challenge was made in a book to evangelical Christians in Britain. It was claimed that churches were emptying, worship was often dull and turgid, and new excitement was needed. An older leader – Revd Gilbert Kirby who was respected by many of his generation – put his neck on the line and endorsed the challenge of a younger man even though he realised that many would mock him for doing so. But the author was my dad, and Gilbert his father-in-law. The older man's support gave the younger man courage. The same remains true today.

There is a much-celebrated secular youth work saying: 'It takes one significant adult to change a young person's worldview, morality and lifestyle forever'. This is an incredible reality. By just one adult bothering to invest in a young person's life you can help that young person realise what really matters. Just one adult can help a young person make informed decisions on things, view the world in a new way and honour themselves and those around them through their behaviour.

Now as a church we are not just here to make bad people good, we are really here to help dead people live, and our churches throughout the West are full of significant adults. Just think how many younger people would be reached and changed if these adults were mobilised. Action that led to not just bad people being made good but dead people living forever!

It is the responsibility of the current adult population to provide a positive example and to mentor the next generation. When the British Prime Minister Tony Blair decided that every young person in Britain needed to have a mentor of some sort it was as if he himself had come up with the idea of mentoring new leadership. Not so – the Bible reveals that people have been practising it for thousands of years. We need a generation of adults who invest in young people wanting them to be all they can be. Just before Elijah was taken up to heaven in a whirlwind, he asked Elisha what he wanted from him before he was taken away. Elisha said, 'Let me inherit a double portion of your spirit' (2 Kings 2:9). This can, at first, sound incredibly arrogant. However, all that Elisha is asking for is the rights of a successor. Deuteronomy 21:17 tells us that the right of the firstborn is a double portion of the inheritance. When Elisha asked for a double portion he was merely asking for what would be required in order to continue the work that Elijah had begun.

Just like Elijah, those of us who invest in a new generation must want them to receive a double portion of anything we might have. One of the key points of mentoring is helping the younger person to avoid many of the mistakes made previously, thus enabling them to be more fully equipped for life. We must want the next generation to be better than us. Why? So that they can see things happening for the kingdom of God that right now seem a distant possibility.

I know too many older folk who are happy to mentor younger people until they seem to be way in advance of them. Pastors who will only let a younger person share their pulpit until that individual portrays a stronger flair, or anointing, for preaching than them. Then all of a sudden the opportunities disappear. For the sake of God and his kingdom we must get rid of this mentality and begin to work together. We need to encourage a new generation with a greater portion of the Spirit as this might lead to us finally seeing a growth and renewal in the church like we have not seen since the Welsh Revival of more than a hundred years ago. The older generations need to be secure enough to want the new to have a double portion, or ten times the portion of the Spirit that they have. After all we are essentially in a family business. It is not about my ministry and me, but instead it must be about God and his kingdom.

I've been very blessed at Youth for Christ to have intergenerational investment modelled to me by my boss, Roy Crowne. He gave me a chance on the leadership team of YFC when I was far younger than most. Few would have taken the risk! He took on someone with evangelical baggage when many others would have preferred me to be out of the way. He did not just leave me to get on with it, he has always been there investing in me, using his experience to save me from costly mistakes – and opening doors for me, which as a younger man I could not do alone. Some of this has been done at a distance, and in other cases I have been given opportunities where Roy and I have shared sermons. I will always be grateful to him for the trust he has placed in me, the support he has given me, and his continued investment. Moreover what he has done for me has meant that whatever I go on to do with my life, and wherever that may be, I will always be looking for ways to invest in and help to raise up the next generation. My own struggles have (I hope) taught me that lesson. For what we model now will be repeated. If we invest in others, then perhaps they may do the same with those that come after them. Of course, if we reject new generations, we need not be surprised if they too, one day, reject us.

What grieves me is to see so many of my peers and the generations below us not being given similar support. I have been given the chance to flourish, while many of my peers have had the opposite experience. I believe it is imperative that the church of Jesus Christ begins to prepare for the future to be not content to reminisce about the past. Personally and professionally it is the responsibility of the church to help people become all that they can be – for tomorrow, not just satisfied to live in the good of yesterday.

We mustn't fall into the trap of believing that it is too soon for some of today's young people. I regularly hear that we should just give them a few years to grow up or become old enough to make a difference. Yet Jeremiah was only a boy, David was the youngest of Jesse's sons, and as we've said, the disciples were a youth group. We need to help these people now. It's not too soon. Let's engage with and assist a new generation. Let's support them where perhaps we weren't supported, give them opportunities where we were denied them and save young people from making the same mistakes we made.

Excuses are easily given and those four wonderful ladies I mentioned above had as many to use as anyone for not being proactive in reaching out to the young. After all, they were praying every day for young people, and from a superficial standpoint they could argue that they had nothing to offer young people. Equally, they had served the church in a multitude of ways both individually and corporately for most of their lives.

If ever there were a bunch of Christians justified in resting on their laurels then it was those four old ladies. However, what I really love about the story is that God proves once more that he uses unlikely people to do crazy things. Over thirty young people hear the message of Jesus every single week because four elderly ladies bothered to try and change things and to make sure the church has a future. The easiest thing for them to do would be to finish their time on earth peacefully. Instead they've got their hands dirty and started to change the world for a new generation.

My great-great grandad preached on his hundredth birthday. My grandad and later my dad headed the

Evangelical Alliance, and both worked with Billy Graham. It's fun to look back on a legacy, yet they both started as young people – and others invested in them.

As you read this I wonder whether or not you are personally committed, practically, prayerfully and financially in nurturing younger people? Are you passing on what you have learned? Are you dreaming with the next generation about what could be? Are you secure enough to want them to have a double portion of anything you've got? It doesn't need to be that difficult. You could have a cup of coffee with a few younger people every couple of weeks to encourage them. You could try and talk to some of those on the outside who no one loves. You could give the church youth leader a financial gift to help with the young. Maybe you could just begin to assume that young people aren't always bad and could really benefit from your help. If you are not currently making things different for a new generation then please begin to invest, as they desperately need your help. You have so much wisdom, experience and life to share. After all, it only takes one significant adult...

Note

1. G. Calver, *Disappointed with Jesus?* (Oxford, Monarch Books, 2004)

CHAPTER ELEVEN

The Pulpit to the Football Pitch (Gavin)

December 26th 2004, will never be forgotten. One of the most terrible natural atrocities of recent times devastatingly hit Thailand and the surrounding area – the Asian tsunami. The world was rocked by images and stories of what had taken place. Anyone who saw the explicit pictures could not avoid being affected, and will probably never forget what they have seen so graphically portrayed. Families were brutally dispersed, lives prematurely ended by the crushing blow of an immense wave, homes and communities ripped apart, and each and every image or news bulletin told yet another story of despair. As the world watched on, we silently hoped that such a disaster would never be equalled.

A few days after the tsunami I found myself going out to do the food shopping. I hate shopping at the best of times and this chore was no different. I wandered through the aisles collecting together the items that Anne had listed on my small sheet of paper. Eventually, and with great relief, I realised that every item on the list was now in my trolley and it was time for me to go to the till. Most of the tills had huge queues, but as I peered down the line I noticed an opening. I rushed along to till seventeen where I found myself to be the very next in line.

Yes, God has broken my heart for young people and I love working with them, but on this day I confess to feeling very tired. As I stared at the spotty sixteen-year-old behind the till I must admit to being in no mood for the intrusion of an impromptu detached youth work moment. He scanned my shopping and I quickly filled up the bags. Avoiding too much eye contact, my gaze came to rest on a black pot by the till that read 'Money for the Tsunami'. As soon as all the food was scanned and packed, I paid the young cashier, and he filled my palm with about £8.00 ($16.00) in change.

As I put the change in my pocket the red-headed cashier squeaked at me, 'Aren't you going to put some money in my pot?' Sensing that I was somewhat taken aback he added, 'Haven't you seen what's happened with that tsunami? Those people need our help.' I recalled to myself the fact that a few days prior to this event I'd given somewhat sacrificially to a Youth for Christ collection for the tsunami. However, here was a young person bothering to make a difference. The least that I could do was to make a minimal supportive gesture. Reaching into my pocket I retrieved £2.00 of the change and put them in his pot, convinced that such a response would suffice.

I turned to leave, but the young lad spoke again, 'That's not good enough. Haven't you seen the television pictures? Children are dying, families need food, and whole villages have been wiped out. You need to give more.' Not one to usually bow to this kind of pressure, today I felt strangely moved. I dug deeper into my pocket and got the remaining £6.00 ($12.00) in change and put it in his pot.

Now by this time I secretly thought he would be really grateful and might even thank me for my generosity. Instead he squeaked yet again, 'Someone who buys as much food as you just have can afford to give more. I must speak up on behalf of all those people who are hurting because of this tsunami.' I felt convicted and compelled to give. I got my wallet out, opened it up, saw thirty pounds in it, took the money out and poured it into his pot.

I turned to leave with my shopping when the young lad changed the topic of conversation. He asked, 'What do you do for a living?' Inside I felt myself thank the Lord that on this occasion I'd been unusually generous towards a charitable cause. 'I work for a Christian charity that works with young people like you,' I said. He seemed taken aback and said, 'You seem a bit normal to do that'. The conversation went on and I had the chance to witness to him a little.

I discovered that this particular young man was uninterested in the church, but he had felt a little of the compassion of Jesus for those poor people affected by the tsunami. That, in itself, provided a real entry point. It was a great opportunity to interact as a Christian with the world! If in normal activities like shopping in the supermarket we find that we cannot take the chance to sow seeds in people's hearts about Jesus then isn't something wrong with our faith? It is when our lives naturally intersect with the lives of others that we need to spontaneously bring Jesus onto the agenda. We may not end up praying the sinner's prayer with them, but we might well have the chance to bring an individual another significant step long the journey from no faith at all to the recognition that there might actually be a God in his heaven, and he might care for his creatures on earth. In other words, it could be possible to get to know him, and perhaps the next 'chance encounter' would take him further.

In Everyday Situations

I've always found sport to be a wonderful leveller, and a great way of meeting people where they are comfortable. It's interesting how, as Christians, we in turn react on a sports field – I think it says a lot about who we really are.

I help to organise a football (soccer) team at my church,

and we play in a Monday night league. The ethos of this
league is evangelistic: while not going so far as to play with
a New Testament in our hands, each team is supposed to
embrace those on the fringes or outside the church. We
were playing in one particular game in which this nineteen-
year-old lad had clearly singled me out. I'm a big guy, and
far from being intimidated, I noted that he was about the
same size and determined to show me who was the boss!
He casually informed me that he was imminently intending
to slit my throat, had been involved previously in intimate
liaisons with a number of people who are close to me, and
made a whole host of other vile promises. Every action he
did close to me on the football pitch was clearly designed
to intimidate. This match was beginning to look like a
rather interesting one.

For a while I had ignored all of his taunts and refused to
be put off. Then we both went in the air for a fifty-fifty challenge. I won the ball and he fell over. As he rose to his feet
it was obvious that his pride was hurt. His whole body language supported the fact that he was now incandescent
with rage. He came stomping over to me purposefully and
punched me twice in the stomach with all his might. I was
left somewhat bewildered as to what to do next. As a paci-
fist I decided to walk away. I'm happy to go in hard for a
tackle but as a Christian am not going to resort to physical
violence. After all we're just a bunch of men running
around after an inflated leather sack.

I am not sure if my decision had any effect on the lad but
I do know that other members of his team were shocked
that I was able to restrain myself and do nothing. Two or
three of them came up to me privately after the game to
have a little word and make it clear that they didn't agree
with their team mate's actions. It again provided the smallest of windows to share the gospel. I might resent the

provocation but have to admit that without it the opportunity just would not have been there.

We desperately need a generation of Christians to rise up who are prepared to live for Jesus in every area of their lives. We must all try to avoid falling into the trap of doing nice things for people without actually telling them why we choose to respond in this way. For witnessing to be effective it must involve both lifestyle and proclamation. Word and deed must go together.

Jesus may have told us that 'Whatever you did for one of the least of these brothers of mine, you did for me' (Matthew 25:40), but he also specifically instructed that we should 'Go into all the world and preach the good news to all creation' (Mark 16:15). Deeds and words give a context to one another, but one alone can never be good enough. It is often argued that the church does more youth work than the state. However, without sharing the gospel as a part of this youth work how are our efforts any different to those that the state would provide? Depriving young people of the spiritual dimension of life does not invalidate initiatives aimed at their physical and emotional well-being, but it does remove the one lifeline which would truly transform their lifestyle for now, and their destiny for eternity.

It was St Francis of Assisi who so famously said, 'Preach the gospel at all times. If necessary, use words'. It seems to me that we have gone to the extreme of attempting to preach the gospel while believing that we never should use words. We have become terrified to declare the name of Jesus because of what we fear people's response might be.

As an evangelist I know the power of the name of Jesus and am only too aware that it provokes a multitude of responses both positive and negative. 1 Corinthians 1:18 sums it up well: 'For the message of the cross is foolishness to those who are perishing, but to us who are being saved it is the power of God'. However, we as Christians must never let the apparent offensiveness of the gospel prevent us from accepting and using the power behind it. I have seen far too many youth missions in which all we actually do is entertain young people without telling them who it is that we live for. By so doing we can deny them that truth which alone will provide the answer to the search of their lives.

Our postmodern Western church can often appear to have become ashamed of the gospel. This is in such clear contrast to Paul, who says in Romans 1:14–16:

> I am obligated both to Greeks and non-Greeks, both to the wise and the foolish. That is why I am so eager to preach the gospel also to you who are at Rome. I am not ashamed of the gospel, because it is the power of God for the salvation of everyone who believes.

Paul would not need telling twice that he was required to share his faith in every context he found himself. Many might say 'but it was different for him' and 'he had it easier'. This is rubbish. By this stage Paul had been engaged in his ministry for almost thirty exhausting years. During this time he had experienced all manner of disheartening things. This apostle had lived through enough trauma, excitement and difficulty to last most people ten lifetimes. He would have had the most compellingly legitimate reasons and argument for giving up on sharing his faith yet in contrast to what you might expect, his enthusiasm did not run out. He knew that if good people stay silent, then bad things happen!

Paul's three bold statements, 'I am obligated' (verse 14), 'I am eager' (verse 15), and 'I am not ashamed' (verse 16) clearly contradict the attitude of many of us who claim to be Christians today. John Stott points out, that too often we appear to regard evangelism as an optional extra, and feel in some perverse sense that if we do engage in it then we are doing God some sort of favour! As if he owes us something for bothering to share! The postmodern mood is often one of reluctance and fear; Paul's was one of eagerness and enthusiasm.[1]

Again many may argue that it was a very different cultural context that Paul operated within. How could he possibly manage to do the same in our postmodern, consumerist, post-9/11 West? The fact is that Paul found himself in a very difficult cultural context where we might also argue that sharing the gospel was untenable. Stott tells us that Rome was perceived as the ultimate symbol of imperial power and pride. People spoke of it in awe and many hoped to visit it on some kind of quasi-pilgrimage at least once in their lifetime in order to simply look and stare in wonder at its beauty. As if this wasn't bad enough, according to tradition, Paul was no beau of a man. He is said to have been ugly and small with eyebrows that met in the middle, skinny rickety legs, a bald patch, bent nose, poor eyesight and no great rhetorical gifts. What could this one man, Paul, hope to accomplish when pitched against the proud might of imperial Rome? Would it not be more sensible to stay away? Or, if he must visit Rome, should he not keep quiet, to avoid being laughed out of town?[2] Paul did not think so. If a man of this appearance in such a city of pride and power believed he could truly change things and share the gospel then what on earth is stopping us?

Whether we like it or not, a number of us may actually be ashamed of the gospel. You may deny this outright as even being a faint possibility but Jesus clearly identified it as a danger when He warned his disciples in Luke 9:26, 'If anyone is ashamed of me and my words, the Son of Man will be ashamed of him when he comes in his glory and in the glory of the Father and of the holy angels.' It is not so

long after this that Peter, the alleged rock, is ashamed of
Jesus and denies him in Luke 22:54–62. We must fight
against fear and be prepared to witness with boldness to a
needy world. For if those who have come to know the truth
are not prepared to proclaim it, then how can we complain
when others do not know the truth? It has wisely been
observed that 'It is better to light a candle than to grumble
about the darkness'.

Some of us are not ashamed. In contrast, what is stopping
many of us from sharing our faith is the fact that we just
cannot accept any inherent value or intrinsic good in either
ourselves or our actions. Low self-esteem is currently pos-
ing a massive problem in our society and therefore in the
contemporary church.

Whenever someone struggles with thinking that they
have nothing to offer my mind always turns immediately to
the feeding of the 5,000 as recorded in John 6. When you
include women and children as well you discover that there
were somewhere between eleven and fifteen thousand hungry people in a field at lunchtime. Jesus asks where they
should buy bread (verse 5) and no one knows what to do
until Andrew finds a boy's packed lunch. He bravely takes it
up to Jesus and says, 'Here is a boy with five small barley
loaves and two small fish, but how far will they go among
so many?' (verse 9). Andrew cannot understand how this
small offering will help, but despite his lack of spiritual
awareness he still knows enough to bring it to Jesus. He
acknowledges that the packed lunch before him is not even
adequate to feed one hungry man, but he is working with a
Jesus who works wonders and so he takes it to the King. As
a result, Jesus feeds the whole field with plenty to spare.

Andrew is probably as surprised as the rest, but he is
beginning to realise that this Jesus can take what seem like
small efforts to us, and use them in incredible ways. He can

take the little that we have to offer and do things with inadequate resources that we would never dream to be possible. The plain and simple reality is that with Jesus on our side anything can happen.

For this reason when we think we have nothing to offer, we must still bring it to Jesus. If we consider that he could use it incredibly then we may well see this belief fulfilled! It is fundamental that as a church we must start witnessing and living out our faith in every environment that we find ourselves in. We must not allow our shame or low self-esteem to stop us. The philosopher Edmund Burke said, 'Nobody made a greater mistake than he who did nothing because he could only do a little.' We need to be a people who avoid that mistake. We must bring our little and watch Jesus use it amazingly. Just as he took a boy's packed lunch and fed thousands of people, he can take our small efforts and use them in incredible ways.

It is of paramount importance that we avoid beating ourselves up by unfair comparisons. There seem to be some people who just tell amazing stories of leading people to Jesus on trains, in parks and all over the place. Such tales make the rest of us feel like we can never live up to these standards. Let me tell you something – we can't! I told the supermarket story and the one from football because I believe that these are accessible to everyone. In both stories the young lads did not instantly fall to their knees, repent and come to Jesus, but perhaps they were helped or moved on a little in their understanding. I was able to briefly witness to them. As a church we need to take these small opportunities as well – these everyday encounters with other people, but where we respond a bit differently, simply because we have Jesus. Believe it or not, life must never be reduced to a competition, with the people of God

battling it out to see which of them can make the most converts, and by any means possible.

You and I may not be the next Billy Graham, but we must
all take up the mantle of sharing our faith in our situations.
We all know 'not yet' (but later to be) Christians who need
to hear the good news from us. We all have a part to play
and can all make a massive difference within a hurting
world. If we each took our mission to the world far more
seriously, then it would be amazing to see what would happen. We just have to realise that our everyday lives provide
us with unique opportunities to reach others.

There is a much celebrated and taught chart of an individual's progress toward conversion called the Engel scale.
This marks out the stages in the decision making process as
an unbeliever begins to consider and embrace Christ. It
begins at −8 with those who have some awareness of a
divine being, and then moves to −7 (some knowledge of the
gospel) and so on until an individual repents and places
their faith in Christ. Engel is making the point that conversion is a process, not a one-off event. It can often take a
number of people to help someone on the journey to faith.
As many as eight or nine independent relationships are
often needed for someone to find faith. We must take seriously our responsibility to the world and start playing our
part in all of this. It may sound technical, but it is gloriously
liberating, because it affirms that bringing an unbeliever
another step on the road toward surrender to Jesus is ultimately as significant in a journey to faith as praying the sinner's prayer with someone as they complete the last lap.

Fundamentally this chapter, and indeed this whole book
has a very simple message: every element of our lives needs
to be committed to making Jesus known. In his book, *The
Life*, J. John writes:

We live in hard times for heroes. There is a cynicism in our culture that eats away at even the most glorious reputations. Almost overnight, selfless geniuses turn out to be selfish fools, great leaders are revealed as insecure bullies and champions of morality are exposed as hypocrites. One of the few figures to survive with their reputation intact is Jesus Christ.[3]

We need to work as a church so that the same can be said in the West in a hundred or a thousand years time. We must not let the name or reputation of Jesus become diminished. We must fight to establish our Lord's relevance and stop an increasingly secularised world from forgetting who Jesus is. As the bride of Christ we need to be mobilised into action, to realise our ambition of touching a small part of our world for Jesus. We must believe that our part is worthwhile and wherever we find ourselves – from the pulpit to the football pitch – we need to share something of the story of Jesus. Every one of us has a part to play in reaching the world with this incredible good news. Let us each make sure that we play it!

Note

1. J. Stott, *The Message of Romans*, (Leicester, Inter-Varsity Press, 1994) p.58
2. J. Stott, *The Message of Romans*, (Leicester, Inter-Varsity Press, 1994) p.58
3. J. John, C. Walley, *The Life* (Milton Keynes, Authentic Lifestyle, 2003) p. 9

CHAPTER TWELVE

Called – to Do *What?!* (Clive)

'**Mum and I are going to America.**' And so the bombshell was dropped. I was to be the new president of World Relief (the US version of Tearfund), and God had confirmed this surprising move in many ways.

Well, he had told Ruth and me, but perhaps not my two sons, Kris and Gavin. The two girls were fine. Vicky was on her way to serve God in India, and Suzy was only thirteen years old, so she could come with us. The two boys were nineteen and seventeen respectively, so they had to stay in the UK for their education.

Gavin asked, 'How can a God of love break up a family like ours?' On the other hand, Kris pithily expressed that if this was the kind of God we loved and served, then he could get stuffed.

As Ruth and I both feared and dreaded, when we left the UK in obedience to the voice of God, our boys left church and left Jesus.

We knew we had no option. As the mother of Jesus pointed out (in my life verse) to the stewards at the wedding feast of Cana in Galilee, they were to 'Do whatever he tells you' (John 2:5). For nine months, Ruth and I were distraught with grief and confusion. We were emotionally shipwrecked, but thankfully, the Lord rescued the boys and brought them back to himself. Sometimes we just have to trust him, even if all odds are against us!

Living in America

'So what's it like over there in America?' Many British friends asked us that question. Arriving in this vast country, I realised I was not ready for the changes. Everything was so big – and so different.

Most folks seemed to think that driving on the other side of the road would present the biggest challenge. What really threw me was being totally unprepared for a situation where – for the first time in my life – people thought that I had an accent. I have to confess that as far as I was concerned, everyone else sounded strange!

Nor were their voices the only thing that appeared funny to me. To my very British ears, these lovely American people appeared to have unconsciously massacred the queen's English. Mysteriously, words had suddenly changed their meaning. When applied to cars, instantly a 'boot' had been transformed into a 'trunk', a 'bonnet' was a 'hood', a 'horn' now became a 'hooter', and the steering wheel was located on the wrong side of the vehicle. Even worse, the whole contraption was no longer powered by a substance called 'petrol', but 'gas'!

I was also unready to face many of the other things that I encountered. For example, everyday issues like climate, currency, sporting occasions, newspapers and shopping malls all conspired together as constant reminders that I was an expatriate Brit, and a very long way from home.

If I needed any further convincing, then the need to always carry photo ID came as a shock. This requirement was coupled with the necessity of facing my first driving test in thirty years (which my children were quite convinced I would fail). Then came the surprise of being expected to remember my social security number, and the phenomenal difficulty of obtaining a green card, after I had been assured that this represented no more than a casual formality. In fact, it took three years to achieve, and I was the president of a relief and development agency with a whole host of refugee resettlement experts on our staff!

Strangely, being a regular visitor to a country can condition an individual to the idea that they would already know what living there was actually like. Words like 'culture shock' referred to something that happened to anyone else, but surely never to them! Now that was one naïve and mistaken idea that I was soon to lose.

Only too soon, I realised how incredibly different things would be in the USA. Sadly, I took much longer to recognise that something different was not automatically inferior – in fact the opposite would often prove to be true.

To tell the truth, I had always been a quintessential Englishman, and I still struggle to make those cultural adaptations that should come as second nature to me by now. Still today some of the folks in our own congregation here in Danbury, Connecticut, will pick up a 'My Prime Minister...your President' comment, which can be unhelpful when trying to build each other up as one family.

My experiences illustrate that a bout of 'cultural blindness' is something we can all occasionally suffer. Living in a different environment does not change us overnight. Time and patience are necessary – from all of us!

I can still remember how I felt a decade ago, when Ruth and I came to America. The move was a huge shock, because, for over forty-five years, I had always been so 'terribly English!' Like many other fellow islanders, I remained pretty proud of being British.

In those days, if you had accused me of being guilty of the sin of nationalism, then a look of injured innocence would swiftly have clouded my features. I would never think of myself as being any more proud of my country than the next person.

When you come from a small island, instinctively, your opinions and perspectives can easily become limited to that small canvas. Retaining an awareness of the big picture can be difficult. When we become so focused on our own situation, we are ignorant of the needs of others in the wider world, and unaware of the extent of their pain. I would be shocked if someone accused me of being blind to my own prejudices, but I was without even realising it.

For some people, a world vision comes naturally. They adapt easily to new cultural situations; they seem almost made for it, but not me! Others may display the capacity to live in a different culture but that trait could not be attributed to me!

I sometimes grimace in embarrassment as I think of God chuckling at the task of relocating such an unsuitable candidate for overseas service. When that challenge suddenly came, I must humanly have appeared to be well qualified for the title of 'the world's most reluctant missionary'.

Escape from Tunnel Vision

Back in those days, my missionary vision was pretty well limited to Scotland, Wales, Northern Ireland and the Channel Islands (located between England and France). I regarded Britain as being my business, and anywhere outside of the four countries of the United Kingdom seemed an area of concern for others.

Now please don't get me wrong. I applauded the activities of missionary agencies and all those individuals involved with them. I wholeheartedly supported all they were seeking to achieve because of their obedience to a biblical command. Looking back, however, I recognise, with embarrassment, my misguided conviction that this overseas 'thing' specifically applied to them, rather than to me. For better or worse, I have to admit being firmly of the opinion that my personal commitment to mission ended at the British coastline. Some of my closest friends would probably have accused me of believing that all useful life ceased at the English Channel. For me to realise that I was wrong was going to take a long time.

You can charge me with being bigoted, prejudiced, or jaundiced in my view of others, and completely myopic in regard to my understanding of what God was doing spiritually around the globe. To all those accusations, I can only answer 'Guilty as charged!'

This tunnel vision reveals a little of my own bias. In question is not just my attitude, cultural conditioning, or individual preference. Undoubtedly, these all have played a part in creating my personal prejudice, but there was, at root, an underlying spiritual dimension. My heart was firmly fixed upon Britain and the way in which it had become such a secular nation that desperately needed to turn back to God.

This compelling, motivational concern was the real driving force that pushed me forward over the years. I believed with all my heart that the living God was going to move again with reviving and life-transforming power throughout the four countries of the British Isles. My single greatest desire was to witness it taking place.

My God was Too British

One day everything changed – and permanently.

Right out of the blue, came a heart-stopping, gut-wrenching, mind-blowing incident. Looking back, the event proved to completely alter the path of my life, and turn it away from any direction I had expected.

The place was Soweto, a sprawling city of small dwellings that had been created by the apartheid regime in South Africa. This sea of shanties was an exclusive homeland for black labour, forcibly imported to perform menial labour in the local industries.

The year was 1996 and I had gone to Soweto with my wife, Ruth, to visit a special friend and his family. Nick Mosupi, who later tragically died in a car accident, was then the Chairman of the South African Evangelical Alliance. He was a gentle giant of a man, a powerful African preacher and leader who cheerfully fulfilled his national role, while being busily engaged in pastoring two churches and continually planting several new ones in Soweto.

As a key leader in the black community, Nick, along with his friends, had been very keen for us to visit a number of new initiatives through which local Christians were seeking to combine social action along with sharing the good news. That day, we had witnessed a number of powerful instances of the church in action, with the most striking laying literally right around the corner.

One night, Ruth and I were actually threatened with a gun while driving in the neighbouring city of Johannesburg, which boasts the unenviable reputation of most dangerous city in the world outside of a war zone. The next day, the two of us were already a little apprehensive, as Nick was carefully winding his way through the narrow streets of Soweto.

We arrived at a bend in the road. Slowing down in order to take the corner, we were suddenly joined by an uninvited guest! A young woman, who was standing at the junction, had taken the opportunity created by our reduction in speed to join us. She had seized hold of the rear nearside door, opened it, and jumped in. Now she was sitting down next to a very surprised Ruth.

The woman appeared to be quite inebriated; a large quantity of alcohol had clearly been flowing in her general direction for much of the day. She sat there, quiet and barely coherent, explaining, 'I am getting into this car because the company here will lead me to God.'

Nick pulled the vehicle onto the verge of the road and proceeded to do just that. He quietly and very simply explained how to encounter Jesus, and the kind of life that the Lord would then expect her to live. He then prayed a short prayer of commitment on her behalf. While Ruth and I sat totally amazed, Nick seemed to regard the incident as all part of a day's work!

After his prayer, he took down the woman's address (in her condition, I was surprised that she could even give it), and then informed her that one of the local pastors would visit her home the next day to pray with her when she was in a more sober condition. He would soon introduce this lady to other Christians in her locality, bring her to her first worship service, and begin to incorporate her into the life of the community church.

This incident was the kind I had long dreamed of witnessing — but in England, not in Africa. On my return to England, however, I faced another surprise.

I was given a special celebration by some of my friends and colleagues to commemorate the twenty-fifth anniversary of my ordination and entry into full-time ministry. The evangelist Luis Palau came and spent the day encouraging younger British leaders. He was then to be the special guest speaker at the evening dinner. As he prepared to address the gathering, Ruth came up to me and whispered in my ear. She told me I was needed elsewhere for a few moments. Apologising to Luis, and putting the proceedings on hold for a few moments, I went out into the lobby of my office building.

Standing there, and looking a little uncomfortable, was a young man who I had never seen before. He hurriedly explained, 'I've been looking for God for the last few weeks. I even went to a church and heard what this Christian thing is all about. But I haven't made a commitment, and I saw the sign on this office door that said this was the "Evangelical Alliance". So can you help me?'

A few moments before, Ruth had heard the doorbell while visiting the 'ladies' room', and having listened to the story, knew that I would never want to miss this opportunity. Out there in the lobby, I led this young guy to Jesus, and then directed him to return to the church he had attended. Feeling on top of the world, I made my own excited return to the reception.

I was amazed that this incident was virtually an action replay of what I had previously witnessed on the streets of Soweto. For many long years, I had dreamed that one day I would see this kind of spontaneous demonstration of the power of God, and had firmly believed that such a move of God would begin in Britain or America. However, God has always been a God of surprises. If ever he had wanted to demonstrate this verse to me, he had done so. 'The wind blows wherever it pleases. You hear its sound, but you cannot tell where it comes from or where it is going. So it is with everyone born of the Spirit' (John 3:8).

I now was forced into the uncomfortable realisation that, although I might be an Englishman by birth, I had actually been reborn into a worldwide church.

The events of that single day in Soweto had created a sea of change for me, a reorientation of my plans for the future, and a shift in destiny that I would never have remotely anticipated. On reflection, I am forced to conclude that nothing could ever be quite the same again. For me, the church, and my God, were getting bigger.

Church...in the Will of God

In the book of Acts and in the epistles, we begin to see the church as it really could be. Like a butterfly emerging from its chrysalis, the real thing became visible. Church began to emerge as a practising community, and I realised that this odd thing called 'fellowship' referred not to mere attendance of meetings, but to the creation of a mutual friendship which would extend to all aspects of life. In Acts, we read that the church had all their possessions in common. Built on that foundation, prayer and ministry could come together, so that fellowship would really become a kind of 'worshipping friendship'.

Some Bible readers have claimed that the 'Jerusalem experiment' (Acts 2:44; 4:32) in the early church was a failure. To me, that statement represents utter unmitigated rubbish. I am tempted to believe that this argument was originally formulated largely as an excuse for Christians, to avoid facing up to the challenge of that kind of lifestyle.

My wife, Ruth, was talking to an African pastor in Malawi who gave her an unforgettable insight into how much we need to challenge one another. He freely confessed that the African churches were often looked down on by their brothers and sisters in North America because of the prevalence of HIV/Aids in the churches, and the somewhat lax moral standards. Then he responded, 'However, if there were a terminal illness that came from materialism, how many people in your churches in the USA would survive?'

This question is poignant. We need to remember that from its relatively humble beginnings, the early church effectively turned its world upside down by cultivating obedience to what Jesus required of each of them.

We need to rediscover this reality again today, and learn

the meaning of belonging to a great family which does more than just get together for meetings.

I have often pointed out the plain and simple fact that Jesus died to give us an abundance of life, not just an abundance of meetings. Much of our time has become meeting-oriented, when the call of Jesus is, instead, to share our lives so that we might serve God together.

Furthermore, sharing of individual contributions or gifts is just part of our service. This family relationship is also intended to transcend all differences created by race, colour, class or culture. In Acts 13, we can see that the Antioch church became a powerful positive demonstration of this kind of togetherness. Their leadership alone was an object lesson in cross-cultural and multi-ethnic partnership (Acts 13:1). It included a black man (Simeon called Niger), and a former member of the most prestigious Jewish religious council, the Sanhedrin (Saul of Tarsus), plus a wealthy man from the island of Cyprus (Barnabas). It also included an African (Lucius of Cyrene), King Herod's own foster brother (Manaean), and presumably the usual sprinkling of slaves. Amazingly, they all met together.

In the early church, both Jews and Gentiles discovered a unity, and even a friendship, in Jesus. This oneness overcame all the anti-Semitism and anti-Gentilism of the centuries. In one miraculous chapter in the life of the church, the two became one in Jesus.

In Christ, all the cultural, political and social barriers began to collapse. The man or woman at the top of the social pile, and their counterpart at the very bottom, met together in the church of the Lord Jesus Christ. They became one in a beauty of human relationships because together they submitted their lives to the Lordship of Jesus Christ. Individually, they did as he told them, and discovered that their agreement to serve him enabled them to walk together (Amos 3:3).

Determining Your Niche

The biggest challenge we each face is finding his role and his will for our lives. How did Paul and Barnabas determine that?

'But two were set apart, and sent out' (Acts 13:2). This commissioning did not mean that Paul and Barnabas were in any way superior, they just possessed the gifts God required for this particular task. Similarly, we should all be prepared to acquiesce to the will of God. He has an individual part for each of us to play in building his kingdom, although we sometimes are confused about our individual gifts.

Ron was converted during the Second World War, and he always wanted to be a preacher. This, he determined, would be his service for God's kingdom. He would join his friends in preaching through a megaphone in outdoor markets and similar locations. The only problem was that, quite frankly, he was not very good at it.

Gradually, Ron came to the disappointing conclusion that he was never going to be a renowned speaker. He found this development difficult to accept, as he longed for God to use him in this way.

Some years ago, I was planning, with Peter Meadows (an old friend and communications specialist), a meeting which we were going to hold in the Royal Albert Hall. This project was ambitious, and one thing we desperately required was someone who could run the box office and sell tickets in the months leading up to the event. Thankfully I remembered Ron.

When it came to administration, he was hard to beat. As

a station manager for British Rail, he had long mastered the art and ramifications of railway timetables, so I thought that the seating plan from the Albert Hall was certainly well within his range of expertise. And so it proved!

I well remember seeing Peter shaking his head with amazement after the event had proved to be very successful. His sense of wonder was not induced by the excellent preaching and music of that evening, nor by the number who had come to faith in Jesus Christ. He was genuinely surprised that Ron had proven able to engineer everyone into the right seat for the event, and even for the overspill performance that had to be arranged for the afternoon.

Subsequently, Ron was kept very busy. I preached at a similar event the next year, and this time Ron managed three events in two days at the Royal Albert Hall. He was concerned that his preaching might be suffering from neglect. A number of us hastened to reassure him that he was utilising his greater spiritual gift responsibly. He really was not a good preacher, but he was a great administrator!

The next year, his reluctant support was enlisted for a tour of thirteen venues around the UK. He only agreed to this on the condition that he could take time off work, and travel with us to personally supervise the box office in each location.

One night he spoke to me with tears in his eyes and said, 'Tonight I heard Luis Palau preach as I could never preach, I watched Dave Pope lead worship, and listened to Graham Kendrick sing in a fashion that I could never emulate. I heard you speak of what God is doing in this land in a way I couldn't speak. And I watched people giving their lives to Christ in a way I have never seen.'

'But I sensed the Lord saying, "Ron, you cannot do these things. But these people whose lives were being changed tonight would never even be here if I was not using the gift I had given to you."'

Three months later, Ron died. That tour was called 'Our God Reigns', and those three words are engraved upon his tombstone. Almost too late, but just in time, did Ron discover that God does not only give gifts to preachers, he loves administrators too!

Ron was one of God's faithful servants who, like the rest of us, had to find out that we all have a job to do and a role to play in kingdom business. We need to discover also that we are not called to be mere passengers or spectators, but participants in all that God wants to do in our world today.

Ron was, in fact, Gavin's grandfather, and my dad. To his memory and in honour of God's amazing provision of Gavin's little daughter Amelie, this book is dedicated. For our God does sometimes link generations together into one great task – standing on the front line of seeking to regain a world for his glory. And to that end we will commit our lives.

Having been started by the American evangelist Billy Graham in 1946, Youth for Christ still exists over 60 years later for the purpose of taking the good news relevantly to every young person in Britain. As one of the most dynamic Christian organisations, its members serve local churches, go out on the streets, into schools and communities, and pioneer new and meaningful methods of reaching young people.

God has used YFC to impact the lives of millions throughout Britain. The staff, trainees and volunteers currently reach over 71,000 young people weekly. There are over 60 local centres, from the Isle of Wight to the Shetland Islands, as well as thousands of churches linked to the movement. Among other things, YFC invests in future evangelists and youth workers, serves in schools and young offenders institutes, provides outreach and discipleship resources for church-based youth work, offers residential opportunities, and places a growing emphasis on peer-to-peer evangelism. British Youth for Christ is part of a wider international family operating in over 120 nations world-wide.

For more information about Youth for Christ in Britain, for prayer points or latest news, please visit www.yfc.co.uk.